MAN AGAINST NATURE

Why Are We Damaging
Our Biosphere?

GORDON CHISM

Published by Avenue Design, Inc.
P.O. Box 512, Fort Bragg, CA 95437
email: kc@avenue-design.com

First limited edition July 2007

For inquiries, contact:
Gordon Chism
P.O. Box 2184, Fort Bragg, CA 95437
email: gchism@mcn.org

Book Design & Production:
Kathy Carl, Avenue Design, Inc.

Writer's Block Coach:
Ann Gallagher

Editorial Support:
Hilair Chism
Bob Winn

ISBN: 978-0-6151-5686-6

Cover Photo
From the NOAA Photo Library
A western hemisphere image from a GOES satellite (artistically enhanced)

*To Kathy, without whose expertise and support
this project would never have taken shape.*

CONTENTS

INTRODUCTION

THE BEAUTY AND DIVERSITY of life on this planet is staggering. From the depths of the oceans to the towering snow-capped mountains, life is everywhere. Trees, bushes, grasses, and flowers take on wonderful forms and colors, while making homes for countless exciting and exquisite animals. We are on the only planet, we currently know of, that is teeming with life. We are blessed to live in this paradise — our biosphere.

But we have a perception problem. In spite of numerous warnings from the natural sciences and irrefutable physical evidence that human activities are damaging this magnificent biosphere, we continue to take nature for granted. I was of reading age when Rachel Carson wrote *The Silent Spring*. She pointed out that we were poisoning nature. I was outraged. But then another dozen springs came along and they were alive with the sounds of nature. In the middle sixties, smog was choking all the major cities. Then laws were passed, car emissions were reduced by ninety percent, and the skies cleared. Scientists in the early seventies warned that we were running out of oil. Ten years later there was an oil glut. WHAT? I was confused. I was conflicted. Was this a case of alarmists crying wolf? I wrapped myself in denial.

The simple truth is that humanity is poisoning the world. Our cities and industries are generating greenhouse gasses. Our waters are being fouled by toxic waste. We are replacing the natural flora and fauna with humans and human-generated plants and animals. We have inadvertently become the animals from hell. Our actions have wounded and unbalanced our biosphere. We have no place to move to. We are hardly acting in the best interests of our life support system.

> As *Einstein* observed: "A human being is a part of the whole, called by us the 'universe,' a part limited in time and space. He experiences himself, his thoughts and feelings, as something separated from the rest — a kind of optical delusion of his consciousness. This delusion is a kind of prison for us, restricting us to our personal desires and to affection for a few persons nearest to us. Our task must be to free ourselves from this prison by widening our circle of compassion to embrace all living creatures and the whole of nature in its beauty."

Why are we doing what we are doing? Scientists are working on hundreds of aspects of human psychology, neurology, sociology, et al. They are generating lots of good micro data but no one is connecting the dots. We have no clear easy-to-understand profile of what a human being is. What motivates us? Why are we behaving in self-destructive patterns?

Where are the modern philosophers the likes of Plato, Aristotle, or Socrates? Where is the intellectual leadership that can guide us past our emotions to self-understanding?

2

Just when we need philosophy to be the middleman between science and emotion, the philosophers have gone off to play mental games with themselves. Philosophy has abandoned its post. What happened to the proposition:

> "Philosophy is the art and law of life, and it teaches us what to do in all cases, and like good marksmen, to hit the white at any distance."
>
> — *Seneca*

Until we have a good idea of who we are and why we are doing what we are doing, we can hardly expect to control ourselves and save our biosphere. Since science is only focusing on the details and philosophy no longer deals with the broad sweep of life, we will have to find the way and the answers ourselves.

I am a lay person rather than a scientist or a researcher, so my essay will not be an academic paper. The overall theme of this piece is a call to informed lay people to share their objective opinions, theories, and ideas in order to come up with an easy-to-understand statement of who we are and why we are doing what we are doing. Researchers have found that, on a given subject, the combined opinions of a few thousand people, selected at random, is more accurate than the opinion of an expert on that subject — hence all the poll-taking. It seems that we do have a useful common consciousness.

This is to be an interactive exercise. The idea is that I give my opinion — my perspective — on who we are and why we are self-destructing. Then after reading my understanding of human life, you give your objective views — your perspective — on the subject. Together with the opinions of a few thousand others, averaging the results, we should be able to generate a useful outside perspective on human motivations and actions (see contact information at the end of this book).

Science has discovered neuroplasticity. The human brain is not permanently hard-wired in one configuration. Our brains can change themselves. Once we have identified our programmed destructive behaviors, we can use cognitive behavioral therapy to change our perceptions. Cognitive behavioral therapy implies that once we identify and acknowledge our self-destructive behaviors, we can consciously assign more appropriate actions to those behaviors. Cognitive behavioral therapy has been used with great success on obsessive-compulsive disorders, phobias, and post-traumatic stress disorders. Our mission is to see, understand, and own our share of the biosphere's troubles.

I have divided this piece into three parts. Part One will be devoted to my view of our behavioral programming — its origin and its influence on our lives. Part Two will be a review of our recent history as viewed through our animal programming. Part Three will be about what we can do to neutralize our current destructive programmed behaviors. I will start with a concise statement of my theory. I will then explain the basis of my reasoning while hopefully generating an outside perspective on our behaviors.

We were able to make it through the cold war without destroying our planet. It has been a little over two decades and we are back on the brink again. With all of our outstanding technical achievements, I feel we have ignored the most important field of inquiry — human nature. We continue to let our animal programming run on automatic — atomic threats, ethnic cleansing, religious wars, pollution, and overpopulation. We must come to know, understand, and work with our genetic programming if we are to save ourselves from ourselves.

PREMISE

WE ARE HUNTER-GATHERER animals with a large brain. Like all animals, we have genetic programming written by natural selection over thousands of generations. When our senses perceive a threat or opportunity, our programmed emotions are triggered, giving us motivation and energy to deal with the situation. My list of a dozen of our primary movers are: fear, status, fight or flight, us and them, religion, sex, faith, denial, violence, hate and vengeance, icons, and love.

Like all the other animals, we live a predominantly reflexive emotional life. Our wonderful large brain and its ability to think things through logically is used in our intellectual and artistic endeavors, but seldom used in our emotionally-driven politics and day-to-day lives. Our lizard brain (limbic system at the base of our skull) has been calling the reflexive shots for over twenty million years. Our cerebral cortex (the wrinkly dome we think of as brain) is only about one hundred thousand years old. Through a kind of grandfather clause, our old animal emotions are still in control and our new big brain has only an advisory capacity.

A human's brain can be usefully compared to a computer. The human brain is hundreds of times more complex and powerful than today's computers but both need operating software — PROGRAMMING — to function. Our human animal programming was written by natural selection over millions of years. Through genetics, our forebears passed on their winning behaviors and strategies to their offspring. Each generation will produce new behaviors. If those behaviors contribute to survival, those behaviors (given about a thousand generations) will be included in our general genetic programming.

For over ninety-nine percent of the time that humans have been around, we lived in bands — autonomous groups of about one hundred and fifty people. The last fifty thousand years is the time that natural selection added the human programming to the primate programming we inherited. Today we have virtually the same behavioral programming that we had twenty thousand years ago. Programming changes very slowly. We essentially have Stone Age brains.

A constant theme of our programming is that we are communal animals. One human is nothing — slow, weak, with no offensive teeth or claws. But an organization of one hundred and fifty people (a hunter-gatherer band), with its handmade weapons, is the most lethal force that nature ever produced. It is best to think of the ancient hunter-gatherer band as a large omnivorous animal. It is easy to see why the great bulk of our emotional behavioral programming has to do with sustaining our communal band. Without the band, the individual is lost.

Each person is born with a unique set of abilities and a personality and temperament type — the genetic hand we are dealt. The genetically encoded abilities and temperament are given expression through our upbringing — our socialization. Snowflakes all seem to look alike from a distance, yet we know that through a magnifying glass they are each unique. And so it is with humans. We look and behave much the same, yet when we look closely we are all unique. This is the thread of tension that runs through a human life — the need to satisfy our unique individual needs through our programmed emotions while maintaining a communal bond with our family, friends, and community.

Together, our genetic abilities and our socialization give us our BELIEF SYSTEM. Our belief system resides in our unconscious and influences everything we think or do. Our belief system is centered on a faith in the status and superiority of our family, band, religion, community, nation, and ourselves. Our belief system is our point of view — our perspective — our world. We are programmed to have faith in, to promote, and to fight for our belief system. A bumper sticker; "I just do what the little voices tell me to do." The little voices are our belief systems.

To protect our belief system from scrutiny by introspection and logical deliberations, we have a set of defenders — FAITH AND DENIAL.

FAITH: Belief that does not rest on logical proof or material evidence.

DENIAL: The refusal to grant the truth of a statement or allegation.

Faith and denial are the blinders that protect us from analyzing our belief systems. It is our animal belief systems that has us blundering around destroying this beautiful biosphere. If we can generate an outside perspective, look at what we are doing to nature and ourselves from a detached outside point of view, we can come to understand and take responsibility for our destructive course of action.

An outside perspective on human behavior sounds like an easy task. Just drop all of our preconceived emotional notions about others and ourselves, analytically look at our programmed responses, and render an objective conclusion. Easy to say; all but impossible to do.

Most communal animals are organized by STATUS and we are no exception. Status means everything to a human being. With status we have self-confidence, the best mating possibilities, the best food, and the most creature comforts. Without status we have self-doubt and depression. This is neither right nor wrong. This is the way we are programmed.

Status is the controller, the arbiter, the organizer, and the catalyst of who mates with whom and who runs the show. Status is the breeder, the bestower of power, and the backbone of each individual's self-worth, self-esteem, and self-confidence. We need to see the direct relationship between one's status and one's self-confidence and make a note of it — a big note. Status is so all-important to a human life that I think we can safely say that the human game is THE STATUS GAME.

"I don't care about status, it doesn't matter to me at all" — DENIAL. We don't think we care about status because in our society, blatant status seekers are considered to be desperate low-lifes. We cannot afford to be one of those low-status losers. While we are trashing status seekers, we may very well be considering buying a BMW.

We are communal animals motivated by fear and status. We come with programmed emotions that are finessed by our socialization. We perceive challenges through our senses. Challenges excite our emotions. Emotions give us motivation. Motivation gives us energy for action. This whole process happens in less than the blink of an eye — not enough time to think it over, only to act.

Even when we do have the time to think, our gut feelings and our intuitions (our programmed emotions) usually override our rational thought. Even when we try hard to generate an outside perspective, we are still seeing through the lens of our belief systems. We never get a truly objective view. The only time we use pure logic is under the auspices of THE SCIENTIFIC METHOD.

In general the scientific method implies that a hypothesis cannot be accepted as true unless the experiment used to prove that hypothesis would produce the same results no matter who performs the experiment. Even when we try to achieve an outside perspective (to be objective), we are seldom successful. The history of science is full of fudged results, biased statistics, and human will rather than proven facts. We can't trust ourselves. Our gut feelings and our quest for status constantly cloud our thinking.

Any hypothesis put forward concerning human behavior may have some general truth, but it is unlikely to stand up under the scientific method. We can guess what people will do, but we can never say with certainty. People are so varied in temperament and genetic predisposition that the repeatable proof of a human action, motivation, or emotion is all but impossible. Human consciousness is in constant flux. We get high, depressed, angry, or horny and react differently to the same set of circumstances depending on what mood we are in — a scientist's nightmare. This is why the scientific community has shied away from the study of our belief systems.

We do what we do because our emotions are excited by perceiving threat, opportunity, or uncertainty in the world around us. In the hostile world of nature, there isn't time to think about what to do, only time to emotionally react. We don't intellectually weigh the pros and cons of our life experiences; instead we instantly respond emotionally. We know this, and our laws make allowances for our reflexive animal emotions. A crime of passion is prosecuted more leniently than one of premeditation. When it comes to our emotions, we are pretty much along for the ride.

Our wonderful large brain has discovered science and science has made our modern world of engines, steel, concrete, guns, chemistry, computers, etc. This has created an emotional animal with unlimited power. All animals are programmed to dominate their niche and that is what we have done. We have taken over the whole planet with our new powers. We have overpopulated the world with people, polluted the biosphere, and caused the extinction of thousands of other species.

To sum up, we are genetically programmed to live as hunter-gatherer animals in groups of around one hundred and fifty individuals (a band). Our unique set of programmed abilities and personality traits, plus our socialization, gives us our belief system — our point of view. Our belief system regulates our emotional responses. Our emotional responses give us our motivations, energy, and actions. Faith and denial protect our belief system from examination and doubt.

Our behavioral programming is so much a part of us that we can't see it. It is my contention that our programming now has us in a "Catch 22." On the one hand, we have come to a time in our evolution where we need to establish an outside perspective on our programming to keep from self-destructing. On the other hand, we are programmed to live rich rewarding emotional lives. Through faith and denial, we are kept from questioning our programming. An outside perspective doesn't come naturally to us. Human beings are still largely ruled by myth. If we are to attain an outside perspective on our emotional programming, we have to work hard for it. Humans would rather believe than know.

The following sections will be an expression of my opinions on human behavior as I attempt to understand why we are fighting nature and destroying our biosphere. I will be dealing in the general rather than the specific. You are welcome to disagree, make suggestions, corrections, or additions. We need all the points of view we can gather.

PART ONE

Our Band Programming

"You can't solve a problem on the same level that it was created. You have to rise above it to the next level."

— Einstein

THE PROBLEM WE ARE CONCERNED with here is that our once-appropriate Stone Age programming, that was written over millions of years of surviving in the wild, has now become self-destructive. What worked well for bands in the wild is not working so well with the large technologically empowered populations in our modern world. The next level we must use to solve this dilemma is an outside perspective on our emotions and our social interactions.

The human brain is composed of about one hundred billion cells interconnected in trillions of combinations to form an unbelievably complex mosaic. As *Charles Sherrington* said: "The brain is an enchanted loom where millions of flashing shuttles weave a dissolving pattern." The only analogy for the human brain that makes any sense is the computer, and even that falls short. Our brains are vastly more powerful, complex, and multifaceted than today's computers.

We are awed by the power of our electronic computers. In seconds, they can make mathematical computations that would take a room full of mathematicians months to solve. Computers, even small computers, make great calculators. But our current computers have a hard time telling a teacup from an apple. The amount of parallel computing power it takes to identify and place an apple and a teacup in a real world context, then locate them in a three dimensional field, is staggering. It has been estimated that this seemingly simple function would take the parallel computing power of hundreds of super computers.

A computer, either organic or electronic, is worthless without a program to run it. With word-processing software, a computer will process words. With game software, we can play games, and on and on it goes from anti-lock brakes to navigating in outer space.

We are so programmed that every action we take, every inclination we have, is directly or indirectly influenced by our genetic programming. Our genetic programming plus our socialization gives us our BELIEF SYSTEM. Our belief system is the foundation from which all our emotional thoughts and actions spring.

The current situation in the Middle East is a good example of our genetic ancient programming overriding our rational abilities by imposing inappropriate animal emotions on a problem that begs for rational deliberation.

The Islamic emotional point of view might go something like this. The First World nations openly violate the main tenants of the Islamic law and religion — the Islamic belief system — the Islamic way of life. The First World nations display pictures of naked women to sell alcoholic beverages. First World nations lend money on interest. First World nations openly brag of their accomplishments and give little or no respect to Islam or Islamic nations.

The Arab and Persian worlds want status and respect. The First World wants oil. The First World gets the oil and the average Arab or Persian gets ongoing humiliation.

RAGE! The Arab and Persian populations are experiencing status rage. They are MAD AS HELL! They are so mad that their extreme elements are willing to commit suicide to strike back at what they view as their tormentors, the mockers of their belief system — the condescending First World.

An outside perspective might go something like this. Most of the Arab and Persian countries are still governed by royals, dictators, or warlords with strong religious foundations. Their nations are usually run by a few rich royals and businessmen, while multitudes live in poverty. The First World is enjoying prosperity. Oil has brought the two disparate cultures into conflict. Human beings are organized and emotionally sustained by their status. The First World has all the international status and the Arab and Persian world has none.

The First World has consistently supported and given military assistance to corrupt Arab and Persian dictatorships in order to secure oil. The Arab and Persian people — the same people who built the pyramids, gave the world mathematics, and beautiful architecture — have been living in poverty, consistently marginalized, degraded, and insulted for the last couple of hundred years. When the World Trade Center came crashing down, the whole Arab and Persian world couldn't help but give out a collective cheer.

I can't watch the tapes of the World Trade Center crashing to earth. I must turn away. I have to leave the room. With just a glimpse of the scene, I get a hot rush of vengeance. I want to strike back — NOW! I go through all sorts of mental scenarios where I smash the evildoers and rid the world of everyone who would do such a thing or applaud such an action. This is my American belief system — my emotional American perspective.

Whenever Bart Simpson gets into trouble, he says, "The devil made me do it." Our devil is our Stone Age programming. We are extensively programmed, just as all animals are. Just as the family cat cannot be trained to stop killing birds and dogs cannot be stopped from marking out their territories, human beings cannot be stopped from playing out their animal programming. From the embattled Middle East to the melting ice caps, our emotional software made us do it. If we don't stop running on automatic, if we don't step back and get some perspective on our now-inappropriate animal programming, we will follow that programming to the letter and self-destruct, taking this beautiful planet with us. To quote Walt Kelly, "We have met the enemy and it is us."

NATURAL SELECTION is the author of our human animal programming. Around the middle of the 19th century, Darwin simply and elegantly explained how all the creatures on earth got to be the size, shape, and temperament they are now. Natural selection, simply stated, is: "Multiply, vary, let the fittest live and the weakest die."

Natural selection doesn't work with a clean sheet of paper. The human body has an appendix that hasn't been in use for millions of years and our poorly-designed back is left over from our quadruped days. Every animal is a modification of an earlier animal and inherits most of the earlier animal's instincts and programming as well as its general physical makeup.

The modifications come from mutations. Every newborn is different in some small way from every other member of its kind. If an animal's mutation improves its fitness (better strength, speed, smell, sight, intelligence, behavior pattern, thought process), that new set of genetic instructions will become typical of that species over time. For example, an animal is born with a new combination of genes that makes it two percent faster afoot than its forbears, which in turn makes it and its offspring five percent less likely to be caught by predators. Given enough time (to let the math work), only the animals with the new genes will still be alive. That is natural selection, an endless development of the survivors through chance.

At the core of our programming is a strong common set of drives that resides in all animals. The drive of life is to survive at any cost, to reproduce and get our genes into the next generation. All animal programming is focused to this end. The point of life is more life.

Yes, we are animals. We are hunter-gatherer primate animals that share ninety-eight percent of our genetic makeup with the Chimpanzee. Due to our programmed faith and denial, we have a hard time grasping the fact that we are animals. In the movie *Elephant Man*, when the misshapen unfortunate is unmasked in public, his plaintive cry, "I am not an animal," resonates in a dark place.

We are emotionally repelled by the idea that we are an animal. Our human emotional programming places us above the animals. The animals are here to provide us with food and sport. "We are the chosen ones. It is us against nature and we are winning." This kind of emotional thinking is another example (like war and ethnic cleansing) of our programming overriding the knowledge we have gained through our experiences and rational deductions. Edmond Burke stated: *"Those who fail to learn from history are destined to repeat it."* We repeat our mistakes, not because we have failed to learn from history, but because we are programmed to produce those behaviors.

Another common aspect of our belief system is intuitive knowledge or gut feelings. We constantly hear "Go with your gut feelings." "Trust your intuition." We have an inner feeling that the all-knowing Gods are communicating with us and giving us the real truth. We know we must follow this divine advice.

This is not the Gods whispering in our ear. This is nothing more than our ancient programming speaking to us through our belief system (the little voices). Our instincts were written by our survival as animals for millions of years. In our modern world, our instincts leave plenty to be desired. We need to question our gut feelings. We need to analyze our intuitions.

A good example of the fallacy of our instincts — our gut feelings — is flat earth. Our senses and gut feelings tell us that the earth is flat. The sun circles the earth. There is an up and a down. We now know that none of that is true. And so it is with a good portion of our subjective notions. When examined with logic and science, there is little or no substance to them.

There are good instincts. When we see a person involved in an injury accident, we instinctively run to their aide. This is good. When we see that a child is lost, we help find the parents — also good. When we get cut off in traffic and want to kill the perpetrator, when we blame others for our mistakes, when we find ourselves using racial slurs, when we support a call to war — these are the times we need to question our gut feelings.

By our very nature we are in a double bind. On the one hand our joy, pleasure, excitement, pride, and love all come from our ancient programmed emotions — our gut feelings. But in the modern world of millions of people, our gut feelings also have us blundering around polluting the biosphere and trying to solve international conflicts with war.

Most of us believe that we are open minded. We feel we are neutral and willing to listen to reason. We are sure that we are altruistic and do our part to make this a better world. NOT TRUE! We are actually closed minded. We have very complex, all-encompassing programming written over millions of years of natural selection, influencing everything we think and do. The things we are programmed to do, put in the simplest terms, are to stay alive at all costs and reproduce. The key to accomplishing these programmed tasks is — STATUS.

Again, status is the organizational framework that holds up our whole life. We often hear, "I care nothing for status." Everyone cares desperately about his or her status. We laugh at middle-aged men with obvious comb-overs, overly made-up women, or a man in a power suit with toilet paper stuck to his heel. They are trying very hard to project and enhance their status but are making fools of themselves. We are much amused. They are losing status and we just moved up a notch.

Status loss is the backbone to most of our humor. Abbott and Costello, the Three Stooges, Jerry Lewis, and on and on to Adam Sandler and Jim Carey. When they do a series of really inappropriate stupid things, we laugh out loud — we are delighted. Compared to them, we are status winners. We instantly feel happy and relieved — our status is safe. We may not always do the right thing in social situations, but compared to the comedians, we never do things that inept.

When people talk amongst themselves about another who isn't present, they tend to be critical. Research has found that two-thirds of conversation is gossip. We are fascinated by other's actions and reactions — hence all the soap operas, novels, and movies. All there is to a human life is other humans. It's the way we are wired.

Since we are subconsciously always trying to support our status and undermine our peer's status, gossip tends to be a little derogatory. "You should have seen Marge. She gushed over the physical trainer like she was a teenager." "George kept shaking the congressman's hand and wouldn't let go." We tend to be experts on the subject of others' lives but seldom honest about our own lives. We use our analytical skills on others' actions and denial on our own.

We can't afford an honest appraisal of ourselves. We must keep our personal sense of status up or our lives will sink. Again, a human life is an ongoing struggle to maintain sufficient status to support a healthy self-confidence. A healthy self-confidence is the key to success, sex, and a sense of well-being.

We are so consumed by our relative status to others that when we say something stupid in a new group of people we are apt to blush. Blood rushes to our face. Our minds are stunned. We can't compose ourselves. We have just lost all the status we were sure we were communicating to others.

Our social status determines our quality of life. With status you get the best mating and social possibilities, the best housing, the best food. Without status you get ignored. We are accorded our status through others. Status (according to our programming) is power, ability, beauty, youth, and energy. We all have a status ladder we are trying to scale — from the big money, big car, big house, to a person who aspires to be on the club's refreshment committee.

Yes, we do have the capacity to employ logic, but the vast majority of the time we use logic it is in the service of our emotional animal programming. We can override our faith and denial and employ pure logic, but the task is so difficult that we must use all the self-discipline we can muster, a twelve-step program, and a strong support group. Even then, it only works hour-to-hour and day-to-day. For example, most everyone at some time or another has been on a diet. Logically it is a simple problem — take in less food, we lose weight. We can't do it. We work hard, make some progress, but soon fail. When our emotional programming says eat, we must eat. Think of the time and opportunities we wasted in school thinking about sex. When our emotional programming perceives a sexual opportunity, we think sex. And so it goes with our whole lives. Our programming gives us our emotions. Our emotions give us motivation. Motivation gives us the energy release that drives our actions. Our intellect has only a weak advisory capacity.

We don't have control of our minds. Our emotions dictate what our minds think and do. How often have you wished you could just turn your mind off and sleep? How often have you wished you had a channel selection switch in your head? How wonderful it would be if you were able to switch your mind to think only about work, family, creativity, your sport, sleep, etc. If only you could click on your depression, anxiety, jealously, fear, or worry, and drag it over to the trash and just get rid of it. But no, we are essentially along for whatever ride our emotions pick up on.

We have a rational side but it is a new arrival on the scene. Our large cerebral cortex (the wrinkly dome) is only about a hundred thousand years old. Our underlying limbic system is over twenty million years old. Our old emotional limbic system is in control and our rational cerebral cortex is the new kid on the block.

> "Much of mental development consists of steps that must be taken quickly and automatically to insure survival and reproduction. Because the brain can be guided by rational calculation only to a limited degree, it must fall back on the nuances of pleasure and pain mediated by the limbic system and other lower centers of the brain."
>
> — *E.O. Wilson*

Throughout our history, the biggest rational advances have been motivated and financed by war efforts. When our programmed animal emotions get us into war, it is usually our intellect — through rational organization and technical innovation — that tips the balance of battle. Our emotions are programmed. Our socialization dampens or excites those emotions, giving us our motivations. Our motivations release and focus our energies.

When growing up in our band, the social rules of the band are learned through the band's shared beliefs. These social rules and group beliefs are given authority by the group's rituals, beliefs in hero ancestors, and supernatural powers. When practiced over hundreds of years, these band belief systems became religions. We have always had religions. Religions give us a time-tested package deal — a personal and band belief system. We don't have to figure out life on our own. Religions give us a one-size-fits-all, ready-made, time-tested belief system.

Our human behavioral software programs were written by natural selection over thousands of generations. We survived the ravages of nature and in so doing, modified our old primate programming into human programming. We adapted to virtually all climates to inhabit every corner of the planet — not just surviving, but dominating the food chain. We lived as human hunter-gatherer animals within the framework of nature just like all the other animals. We are and will remain, for thousands of years to come, programmed as human hunter-gatherer animals.

Today, we are essentially the same people genetically that we were twenty thousand years ago. If a baby born to a Stone Age band could be transported to today, he or she would fit right in. He could go through our school system, get a job, and live a modern life. The same is true for the corollary. If a twenty-first century baby was placed in an ancient hunter-gatherer band, she would seamlessly assimilate.

Even with our advances in technology and changes in lifestyle, we are still programmed to be Stone Age people living a hunter-gatherer mode of life in bands of around one hundred and fifty individuals, living one season at a time. That's what we are programmed to do. That is the only thing we are programmed to do.

Our belief system is composed of our genetic gifts and our socialization — our upbringing. Our socialization is provided for in our programming. We have encoded instructions to absorb and adopt the ways of the band we are born into. Stories, heroes, myths, legends, the supernatural, and spiritual beliefs band us together.

These beliefs, no matter how weird they may seem to an outside observer, become the emotional glue that holds our band together. For example, if a child, with his unique genetic makeup, was raised in a working class Texas family whose religion was fundamental, politics were Republican, sports were guns, hunting, and football; his or her socialization (and belief system) would be quite different if that same child had been raised by a middle class Democratic California family who was into the Sierra Club, golf, and soccer.

Again, our genetic behavioral programming plus our upbringing and socialization gives us our belief system. Our belief system is our unconscious point of view — our perspective on the world we live in and depend on. Without a belief system we would perish. A belief system is the rock on which we build our social life. We are all unique. Unless we establish an agreed upon set of ideals and behaviors, we will not be able to sustain band cohesion. Unless we work in the same direction, the band will dissolve. Without our band support system and protection, we couldn't have survived in the wild. Our belief system is who we are individually and communally. Our band — our support group — must all be on the same page, singing the same tune. We must establish a common bond — a shared belief system — to effectively stay alive in the wild.

We need to understand what the broad sweep of our programming is — how we successfully acted and interacted in our natural environment twenty thousand years ago. These are the successful behaviors that kept our species alive for the last fifty thousand years. We also need to see how our hunter-gatherer programming is playing out in our current lives. If we are to win this all-important battle to save our beautiful planet, we must know our enemy.

In their book, *The Imperial Animal*, Lionel Tiger and Robin Fox show us a window into the day-to-day lives we led twenty thousand years ago. In the ten short statements presented below, the authors describe the workings of the hunter-gatherer economy and the behaviors that won out in the millions of years of Darwinian struggle. This is who we are programmed to be in the sense of our day-to-day living:

> "In bands of about one hundred and fifty individuals, we lived our lives with a sexual division of labor — gathering by the females, hunting by the males. The business of the band was conducted through the cooperation of males in the framework of competition between males.
>
> 1. The band is small-scale, face-to-face, and personalized.
>
> 2. Foraging by the males, the cooperation of the males in the framework of competition between males. [sic]
>
> 3. The band is based on a sexual division of work requiring males to hunt and females to gather.
>
> 4. The band is based on tool and weapon manufacture.
>
> 5. The band is based on a division of skills and the integration of these skills through networks of exchange (of goods, services, and women).
>
> 6. These are networks of alliances and contracts — deals — among men.

7. The band is involved in foresight, investment, judgment, risk taking — a strong element of gambling.

8. The band is involved in social relationships based on a credit system of indebtedness and obligation.

9. The band is involved in a redistributive system operating through the channels of exchange and generosity; exploitation is constrained in the interest of group survival.

10. The band bases status on accumulative skill married to distributive control — again in the interest of the group as a whole.

It is important to see all these factors as integrated into the hunt. They are social, intellectual, and emotional devices that go to make up an efficient hunting economy, in the same way that muscles, joint articulation, eyesight, intelligence, etc., go to make up the efficient hunting body. They are the anatomy and physiology of the hunting body social. It is a system of the savannas and the hunting range, and it is the context of our social, emotional, and intellectual evolution."

The above quote from The Imperial Animal, describing a hunter-gatherer society, was compiled through research. What this research is saying is that we are genetically programmed to conduct the business of being human in these patterns.

Now, let's go back over this list of social behaviors again and take them one statement at a time and see what insights into our social programming we can glean. Remember, all these statements are what we are programmed to do. It isn't right, it isn't wrong; it is how we are programmed to behave and we can't easily change it.

1. *The band is small-scale, face-to-face, and personalized.*

Our human software is a program that assumes that we are living in a group of around one hundred and fifty — a band. About one hundred and fifty people — that's all the people we are programmed to deal with. If we examine our own lives, we see that we have in our band two or three close friends, about one hundred or more relatives, acquaintances, co-workers, and celebrity idols. For ninety-nine percent of the time that we have existed as a species, only a handful of people ever knew, or even met, more than two hundred others in their lifetime. We are designed and programmed by natural selection to live in an insular society of around one hundred and change.

In today's global village of six billion, our software is on constant tilt — our social gyros are tumbling. Our private lives are constructed to operate from a foundation of a strong sense of security and identity. In a band of a hundred and fifty, every person is needed; every person's talents are needed, appreciated, and depended upon by the rest of the band. Identity is a given in a band. Every member knows every other — who their parents, grandparents, uncles, brothers, and sisters are. Since they all lived together and depended on each other, a sense of support and security was guaranteed. Our software has no provisions for coping with cities of hundreds of thousands. We only have the programming to deal with about a hundred and fifty others. Today we all suffer to some degree from security and identity anxiety.

"Face-to-face, and personalized." We may live in cities of hundreds of thousands but our lives are the same as the ancient band days, only now our band lives are afloat in a sea of humanity. We still relate to about one hundred and fifty people. It is all we are programmed to do. The human mind cannot conceive of a thousand individual people; anything over a couple of hundred and they become an abstraction — a statistic. Every human, from the president of the United States to the clerk at the convenience store, knows and relates to about one hundred plus other people.

We can't relate to the plight of a million starving people. We can only say, "That's too bad." But if we are shown one pretty five-year-old, obviously under-nourished, girl named Maria, we can enlarge our band by one and feel and participate in the full emotional impact of the situation. To quote Stalin, "One death is a tragedy, a million deaths is a statistic." And so it is with all the facets of our lives. It is the personal one-on-one, face-to-face we feel about emotionally. We generally deal with the world of millions as a series of figures.

When we lived as hunter-gatherers in bands of one hundred and fifty, our life was personal one-on-one, and face-to-face. We could see, touch, and smell all the things, events, and people that impacted our lives. Today the vast majority of the things, events, and people that impact our lives are distant abstractions. We are trying to deal with this abstract existence through our personal one-on-one programming. No wonder we feel at times like fish out of water.

This is not necessarily all bad. Our modern anxiety keeps us working harder and longer to get the status and group acceptance that was a given in our old band. Humans, like most animals, are creatures of adversity. Without tension and anxiety to excite our emotions, we tend to lose focus and interest in life.

2. *Foraging by the males, the cooperation of the males in the framework of competition between males. [sic]*

This statement explains a whole lot of male behavior in our society. In a Stone Age band, the males hunted in groups of three to five and in larger war parties of ten to fifteen. Sound familiar? A basketball team, a football team, soccer, hockey, baseball, cricket, and on and on to shooting some hoops or hanging out at a local sports bar — "the guys."

Men are programmed to congregate and pal around with three to five guys and be part of a larger group. In our ancient band days, the activities were hunting and band warfare. Today it is motorcycles, golfing, tennis, watching TV sports, hunting in the woods, or hanging at the bar — with the guys. The pecking order is well-established from the leader down to the last alternate. They have a bond. They cooperate to form a group that has identity and power, but they also compete among themselves for status within the group. It's the backbone of the Stone Age hunting party — the sports team, the ghetto gang, and the Army squad. It is also the way men are programmed to behave. They can't help it. Their software makes them do it.

The final arbiter in nature has always been, and still is, physical violence — the ability to dominate or eliminate an adversary. With a twenty-five percent pound-for-pound advantage in strength, plus a naturally larger frame, man holds a physically dominant position over woman. So, the hunter-gatherer society was male dominant. That was the way our software was written for conducting Stone Age business. Ironically, modern business seems to favor the female-programmed ability to cooperate, listen, get along, and compromise.

3. *The band economy is based on a sexual division of work requiring males to hunt and females to gather.*

Recently the feminist movement tried to promote the theory that the differences in the sexes were primarily socially generated. The women's movement made the fundamental error of judging our programming as being one-size-fits-all, male or female. Male programming and female programming are quite different. The feminists were judging without understanding. They didn't see that it isn't right, it isn't wrong — it just is.

Male and female roles were written into our programming hundreds of thousands of years ago. This arrangement of males hunting, females gathering and keeping camp is simply the most efficient allocation of labor for human survival on the savanna. For starters, women are smaller and physically weaker than men. That's why we have different events for men and women's athletics. This is not to say that women can't hunt; it just means that men are better equipped to do so. That edge in size and physical strength could mean the difference between starvation and survival in the wild.

There are many spin-offs in this part of our software. Recent studies have shown that men and women's brains are very different. Women are better at language than men (research has found that on the average women talk three times as much as men do). Women cooperate while men compete, and they have a deep love of children. All of these characteristics dovetail with the gather-tend-the-children-keep-the-fire-burning role in women's programming.

Women have a social program that is more inclusive. Women hang out in larger groups — women's support groups, exercise classes, art classes, bowling teams, golf and tennis clubs; any group activity where they can gather around to exchange information and enjoy being together.

That's what women are programmed to do — hang out around the hub of the social child-raising communal life of the band and make it all work.

4. *The band economy is based on tool and weapon manufacture.*

This line of the human hunter-gatherer economy marks the beginning of our departure from the constraints of nature's framework and the laws of natural selection. While the other animals survived by becoming faster, stronger, and quicker, humans became smarter, smarter, and smarter. About two million years ago we had a brain capacity of about five hundred cc, comparable to a chimp. By the time we evolved into Stone Age hunter-gatherers (about one hundred thousand years ago), our brain capacity had almost tripled to around fourteen hundred plus cc. Our big brain is energy intensive. It takes 20% of our energy to run it, while other animals require only about 5%.

Our new mental capacity, together with our wonderful opposing-thumb-four-fingered hands, made us toolmakers extraordinaire. Without our hands, our mental capacity could never have achieved the expression it has enjoyed. Scientists believe that whales may possess intelligence close to our own, but without a means to create tools to leverage their intelligence, they are dead in the water.

This ability to make tools more than made up for our lack of dagger teeth and claws and we were off. This programmed need to create with our minds and hands is what has taken us to the edge of understanding the universe. It has also placed unlimited power at the disposal of an animal that is programmed to expand its numbers with no regard for other life forms. This is what all animals are programmed to do. This is what the human animal is still doing.

5. *The band is based on a division of skills and the integration of these skills through networks of exchange (of goods, services, and women).*

This part of our programming still works well. We all have different skills, capacities, and talents, and we trade our strengths for the strengths of others in our band. It is the basis of communal effort and commercial enterprise; "two heads are better than one."

Now to the part about trading women along with goods and services. Stone Age bands, by definition, had an inbreeding problem. Insular, isolated, and close-knit, the band was always in danger of inbreeding and genetic stagnation. Anthropologists have found that all primitive bands had provisions for the exchange of women with neighboring bands and taboos on brother-sister sex.

6. *These are networks of alliances and contracts — deals — among men.*

The "networks of alliances and contracts — deals — among men," is our political programming. This is the horse trader part of us; we negotiate for everything in our lives, personally and for our band. A breakdown in negotiations could result in violence deciding the matter. Now, as in the hunter-gatherer days, talking is less hazardous than fighting. The "among men" part was appropriate in the bush in that men added a physical threat component to the bargaining table.

Today, women are proving to be every bit as adept at forming alliances and negotiating contracts as men are. Under our laws, physical intimidation no longer has an effect on the outcome of business transactions, whereas a willingness to compromise and listen has become a more significant networking requirement.

7. **The band's economy involves foresight, investment, judgment, risk taking — a strong element of gambling.**

Foresight, investment, and judgment are prominent components of our success as a species. Our large brain gives us the ability to reason a probable set of future occurrences from past experiences and spend present resources for a better tomorrow. This put us ahead of the other animals. In a calm state of deliberation, we can learn from the past and avoid future mistakes instead of depending completely on our instincts. It is when we are challenged that we downshift into our animal "fight-or-flight" programming.

Risk taking and gambling are a strong part of our software. We get such a strong programmed rush from winning that we generally forget the losses. From the state lottery to the Las Vegas strip, people line up to gamble and the vast majority of them have lost many times the amount they have won. They will do it again and again. The programmed rush of pleasure that most people receive from tempting fate and getting away with it is so strong that dull logic usually doesn't have a chance. We gamble to prove our favor with the Gods. We can't help ourselves; we are programmed to do it.

Most of us have an unshakable belief that "The Great Spirit" knows us personally and has chosen us for greatness and all we need to do is take the right chances at the right time and one day we will hit it big. It is our programming's "carrot-on-a-stick" that runs through our emotional make-up — "A faint heart never won a fair lady."

It is also why controlled capitalism is emerging as the world's choice of economic systems. The hunter-gatherer economy and modern capitalism are the same games played on different fields. It is comfortable and familiar.

Today we still compete for our personal status while earning our living, just like in the bush.

8. *The band economy involves socialrelationships based on a credit system of indebtedness and obligation.*

We all have an intuitive sense of what is owed to us by others. Studying chimps, scientists noticed that each individual knew how much each of the other chimps had eaten of the group's common food supplies. Days later they would shun or punish a chimp that had taken more than his fair share. It is part of our communal Darwinian software handed down to keep us in cohesive groups for our mutual protection. We are programmed to keep the band as egalitarian as possible. We socially punish those who try to take more than their fair share. It is this spirit of "we are all in this together" that keeps our band strong.

Credit is the backbone of our current societies. We instinctively understand the concept of borrowing and paying back. We also have a strong aversion to someone borrowing and not paying back. When others don't repay their indebtedness, we get a strong emotional reaction. This is our old programming at work. Taking without giving a commensurate amount back breaks the ancient communal bond, leaving the Stone Age band weak and vulnerable to internal bickering and outside attack.

9. *The band economy involves a redistributive system operating through the channels of exchange and generosity; exploitation is constrained in the interest of group survival.*

This is our reciprocal altruism gene set — "I'll help you if you help me." A computer model was built to see if reciprocal altruism was a winning social strategy in a band situation. Yes it is. We are programmed to help others so that we will have the security of other's generosity should we get injured or have poor luck in the hunt. This is more glue to keep the band pulling together — all-for-one and one-for-all.

Exploitation is only a viable ploy if there are expendable people around. Since a band is a small, personal, one-on-one group, it was inappropriate to exploit another band member. Exploitation is a relatively new problem of the post-band periods with the interaction of large populations.

10. *The band bases status on accumulative skill married to distributive control — again in the interest of the group as a whole.*

In Stone Age bands, the man who gave the most to other members of the band was accorded the most status. He would need to have great energy, talent, and skill in order to acquire enough to give to others. Hunter-gatherer bands didn't have employer-employee relations. Whatever a man gave to others would have to be from his own efforts. He would have earned the status. What a great boost to the welfare of the band to have all the members competing for status by giving to all the other members of the band!

It is all too obvious how this has changed in our present large populations. Since "one-on-one personal contact" is only a sometimes thing in large populations, status switched from the person that gave the most to others, to the person who controlled the most power.

An extension of our status programming is band leadership. With enough status, leadership is there for the taking. If a small band were to survive the ravages and uncertainties of nature, there would be times when there could be no questions or debates. Immediate decisions by a single leader would have to be made and acted on. This programmed need for unquestioned obedience to our leaders has been encoded into our software over millions of years and is now hard-wired. History has too many examples of this now-inappropriate software in action — Hitler, Stalin, Saddam Hussein, and on and on.

> "It is important to see all these factors as integrated into the hunt. They are social, intellectual, and emotional devices that go to make up an efficient hunting economy, the same way that muscles, joint articulation, eyesight, intelligence, etc., go to make up the efficient hunting body. They are the anatomy and physiology of the hunting body social. It is a system of the savannas and the hunting range, and it is the context of our social, emotional, and intellectual evolution."

The above summation by Tiger and Fox of the hunter-gatherer economy is worth restating. Through their analogy, they show that hunting and gathering are not only what we are programmed to do physically, but also what we are programmed to do socially, emotionally, and intellectually. It is our job. It is what we do. It is the only thing we have the software to do.

Our Personal Programming

O UR SENSE OF BELONGING and oneness is so strong in our communal programming that we assume we are all alike. "I know exactly how you feel." If only we had a dollar for every time we have heard that one. No, they don't know exactly how you feel. We look so much alike (two arms, two legs, a body, and a head) and we follow the same rules, eat the same food. We must be the same. No. According to the mother-daughter team of Myers-Briggs, there are four general types and sixteen specific character and temperament types. Each is clearly different and distinct from other types. Myers-Briggs, drawing on work done by Jung, Adickes, Kretschmer, Adler, Spranger, and Hippocrates came up with the type indicator test. The U.S. military and many corporations use character and temperament type tests to best utilize their employees.

The team of David Keirsey and Marilyn Bates wrote *Please Understand Me* based on the work of Myers-Briggs. In their book (I recommend everyone read it), Keirsey-Bates draw sketches of each of the types and how they interact with others. They employed Greek mythology in their explanations of the four general types, naming them Dionysian, Epimethean, Promethean, and Apollonian. To work the four types into my theme of hunter-gatherer software, I have renamed them DOERS, KEEPERS, THINKERS, and DREAMERS.

Taking the statistics generated by the research done by Myers-Briggs, a profile of a human population can be drawn. All human populations, regardless of nationality, geographical location, or ethnic makeup, have about the same proportional balance. The character-temperament types are given at birth. One's type is not the result of breeding. Two Doers do not necessarily produce another Doer. Any man-woman combination can give birth to any type. Types seem to be randomly assigned, but are actually assigned proportionally within band populations. Your personality (character-temperament) is your first birthday present.

The human landscape is populated with personality types roughly in the following manner. Within the various character-temperament types, there is an equal chance of being male or female. Seventy-five percent of a given population are extrovert and twenty-five percent are introvert. Forty percent of the population are Doers, forty percent are Keepers, ten percent are Thinkers, and ten percent are Dreamers. Character-temperament types share intelligence equally. No one type is more intelligent than another.

It is easy to see that in a democratic society, the Doers and Keepers, who are close to eighty percent of the population, will control the voting. The Thinkers and Dreamers, while influential behind the scenes, will have little impact on the actual voting.

In the context of the hunter-gatherer model, humans have different types of individuals suited to do different tasks, just as bees have to keep their hive operating efficiently. The bees have drones, workers, queen tenders, etc., and humans have Doers, Keepers, Thinkers, and Dreamers. Now let's take a closer look at each of the four basic types of human character and temperament — how they act, react, and interact in the context of the hunter-gatherer band in the wild and on the contemporary scene.

Doers

This group is the most visible part of any population. Doers generally have good dispositions, positive outlooks, and like to have a good time. They usually live in the moment, are easy to make friends with, and act impulsively. "Now" is their only time-frame. They tend to ignore the past and the future. They must have the freedom to act without constraints. They don't make elaborate plans because they have to be free to answer the call of their urges.

Doers enjoy the unexpected, the spontaneous, the call of the wild in whatever form it takes. They are super realists who seldom deal with the subtle or the abstract. They prefer to deal with what is rather than what has been or what could be. They are compulsive in their actions and can keep performing when other types would become fatigued or bored. They look on material things as being expendable. Money is to spend. Food is to eat. People are to enjoy. They are generous and expect generosity in others. In short, they are the stuff that our action heroes are made of — John Wayne, Ellen DeGeneres, and Michael Jordan are good examples of Doers.

Since they comprise forty percent of the population, we all know and are probably related to a Doer or two. They are the types that show up for an appointment two hours late and can't understand why you are upset. They meant to be on time but they met this guy and . . . They are usually broke, yet have an impressive car. They are the prototypes for, "what you see is what you get." To know them at all is to know them well. They are generally charming and exciting but are apt to disappoint when others put expectations on them. They must be free to act on impulse.

Doers are the virtuosos in sports, music, and art — any performing discipline. While other types struggle to find the time and commitment to practice, the Doer just does it and does it and does it. They act on compulsion to the point of obsession and end up masters, while the rest of us work hard to master our chosen endeavors and never get there. They don't care so much if their actions produce anything for the future. They just want to be seen chance-taking with style and freedom. They are great in a crisis. They love the excitement, the spontaneity, the chance taking, and the action.

The Doer's contribution to the ancient hunter-gatherer band can readily be seen. They are chance-taking, in the now, looking for action — everything a warrior needs for the hunt and the protection of the band. In our contemporary society, they are athletes, firemen, policemen, performing artists, craftsmen, pilots, drivers, operators, construction people, and soldiers — any occupation that provides movement and action and chance-taking.

Keepers

At forty percent of the population, Keepers are the other large chunk of society. The Keeper is the ant to the Doer's grasshopper. The Doer must be free to act. The Keeper must be obligated to serve. The Doer uses, the Keeper maintains. Doer spends, Keeper saves. They are exact opposites. To know one is to know the other.

To the Keeper, life is defined by one's heritage, the organizations one serves, and a strong sense of right and wrong. To do for others, preserve traditions, and earn a place of respect in the hierarchies one serves — these are the things of value. The Keeper has a membership lust and a longing for duty — to be a giver and caretaker. Fundamentals, history, standards, responsibilities, social norms, serving the community, institutions, honors, titles, traditions, ceremonies, rituals — all the strong fibers that make organized society possible are the domain of the Keeper.

It is a very good chance that you have a couple of Keepers in your family. They are the ones who organize the family get-to-gathers, belong to service clubs, and work harder and longer than they are required to at work. They always clean up after parties no matter who gives them. They generally have a bit of a negative outlook on life, feeling something is about to go wrong and a vague feeling of guilt over the things they feel they should have done. They also feel under-appreciated and are usually right. They are the people we turn to when we need something done because we know they will not only do it, but will do a good job. They are the backbone of society — the corporation, institution, club, and family. They are the glue that makes our communal life possible.

Keepers give so much and work so hard for the common good that it is difficult to find fault with them. If they do have a downside it would be their inflexibility, intolerance, and need to control. They also have a strong reluctance to change. The Keeper's contribution to a hunter-gatherer band is obvious. They would see to the firewood, meal preparation, stores of food, rituals, and traditions. They were the social structure of the ancient band. In our modern world, they are the lawyers, accountants, middle managers, teachers, medical workers, political workers, and office workers — anyone that works to support and maintain the status quo.

Thinkers

Thinkers are a minority in the population at about ten percent. To other types, the strong Thinkers seem cool, aloof, and arrogant. Mental powers are the end-all and be-all of existence to the Thinker. To understand, control, predict, and explain — that's the meaning of life to a Thinker.

As the Doer must perform and the Keeper must serve, the Thinker must possess knowledge, abilities, precision, and comprehension. The Thinker must have all his ducks in a row and is constantly on his own case to improve, know more, and master new mental skills. This self-critical drive to find the truth behind the truth can spill over into the Thinker's social life, making those about him feel inadequate and intellectually inferior. Thinkers love the complicated, intricate systems and patterns of mathematics and the sciences. They are also drawn to puzzles and word games, delighting in their mental challenge.

In their communications with others, Thinkers tend to be precise and to the point. They refuse to state the obvious and seldom repeat themselves. They have composure and self-control and expect it in others. Thinkers are not swayed by other's status. What others have to say must hold together on its own.

A perfectionist in work and play, the Thinker never lets himself off the hook. Thinkers, more than the other types, are susceptible to bouts of depression — so much to know and learn, so little time. When spending time with a Thinker, people are struck by the Thinker's constant need to be working. They are seldom without books, projects, plans, and places to go. The future is where the Thinker wants to be. The past and the present are of little or no consequence.

In the hunter-gatherer band of one hundred plus, there would be only a dozen or so Thinkers and probably only one or two gifted Thinkers. Since the Thinkers stand aloof, are not swayed by authority, and must understand all things through personal observation, they were very valuable to the band. They were the unemotional observers of events in an emotionally charged environment. The Thinkers have been the great leaders of history — the great Generals who could see the truth of a situation through the fog of emotional reactions. The Thinkers were the warrior leaders and the great chiefs of hunter-gatherer societies.

In our contemporary society, the Thinkers are the scientists, engineers, political strategists, and architects. Their constant probing into the truth of things has resulted in all of man's technical achievements. The Thinkers are the authors of our modern technological world.

Dreamers

Like the Thinkers, Dreamers comprise only about ten percent of the population. Dreamers are as obsessed with understanding the human spirit as the Thinkers are obsessed with understanding the physical universe. As the Thinkers are interested in things, the Dreamers are interested in people's interactions and motivations. Since Dreamers are people, they are in the somewhat odd position of being obsessed with themselves, their motivations, and their actions — their self-actualization.

Dreamers are sensitive to the subtleties of life and the most empathic of all the types. They are often more intuitive about others emotional distress than the others are themselves. Dreamers seem very easy to know, but this comes from the Dreamer's ability to see and provide what others want. Friends report that they have been around a Dreamer for years before knowing them well. The personal quest of the Dreamer is to be authentic, to be real; to have unity, uniqueness, and meaning. Dreamers are driven by an inner need to understand the meaning of life.

In modern life, Dreamers are the creators of fine art and the writers of poetry, plays, novels, and movies. They are always exploring the whys of human motivations, actions, and interactions. They are about one third of our teachers and are the majority of our clergy. Dreamers also make up the vast percentage of psychiatrists and psychologists, the backbone of the mental health establishment. Dreamers want others to realize their potential and are willing to help wherever they can. In the hunter-gatherer band, the Dreamers were the Wisemen, the Shamans, the Oracles, the Medicine men. The Dreamers were the middlemen between the Gods and the band — the seers of the future.

Reviewing the profiles of the character and temperament of the Doers, Keepers, Thinkers, and Dreamers, we can see how natural selection wrote an indispensable role for each type to play in the hunter-gatherer drama. Each is a specialist and their relative numbers reflect the nature of their mission. The Doers were needed in large numbers to hunt and defend. The Keepers were needed in equally large numbers to organize, maintain, and conduct the business of the band. Then the Thinkers and the Dreamers were needed to see the big picture — to look into the past and the future for evidence of what the best next move of the band should be.

If you don't feel that you are exactly one of the four types of temperament and personality (Doer, Keeper, Thinker, Dreamer), you are not alone. Few people are a pure type. Like anything in nature, human personality types are far more complex and interconnected than we can imagine. Most people are a mixture of a little bit of all the types, but do have a strong bias toward one of the four types. (If you want to know more accurately what your type is, there are sixteen subtypes explained in the book *Please Understand Me*.)

Let's review what we have so far. Human beings are hunter-gatherer animals with an outsized brain. Like other animals, we have extensive programming or operating software. Our programming was written by the survival of our primate forebears over tens of millions of years; our uniquely human programming was added in the last fifty thousand years. Basic animal programming changes slowly (on the order of a thousand generations to make small changes). Therefore we have essentially the same general programming, as a species, that we had twenty thousand years ago.

Our ancient programming was predicated on our living in groups of one hundred and fifty. We still only have the programming to interact with around one hundred and fifty others — our family, friends, and coworkers. Our one-hundred-plus people will come and go, changing over time, but our band cannot expand into the thousands, let alone millions.

In general, our genetic programming is fight-or-flight animal programming — fear, status, US AND THEM, sex, and violence. Our programming has us competing for sex, status, and leadership. Our uniquely human programming is centered on religion, faith, denial, icons, and the supernatural. We created gods and spirits to explain the whys of nature and life and to assuage our fear of the unknown.

Our SOCIALIZATION (upbringing) gives shape and direction to our genetic programming. Every human society has a set of social behaviors, icons, ancestor heroes, and Gods that give the society cohesion and identity. Our genetic programming, shaped by our socialization, gives us our BELIEF SYSTEM. Our belief system is our perspective on life. It is our rock, our personal set of rules, rituals, and Gods that reside in our unconscious — our religion. Our band's religion is our overlapping belief system, the gyro stabilizer that keeps us and our band going in the same direction, believing in the same things. Our RELIGIONS give us a one-size-fits-all belief systems. We come into this world with a strong programmed need to adopt the belief system and religion of our society. These beliefs form our identity and we will fight to the death, if necessary, to protect our society's perspective.

Our EMOTIONS are the action triggers that reflexively give us motivation and energy for our programmed needs (food, sex, and status). Every animal lives an emotional life. Only humans can question their animal rush of emotions and make logical decisions. Unfortunately, logic and reason are the weak younger siblings to our emotions and are seldom used. It is useful to think of a human as a consciousness hitchhiking a ride through life on an animal.

Human beings are organized by STATUS. Status is the common thread running through the human drama. Status regulates sex, leadership, self-esteem, and self-confidence. Everyone is concerned about his or her status. With status, we have opportunities for sex, leadership perks, and a feeling of well-being. Without status, we get rejection and depression. It can be said that a human life is a quest for and the maintenance of his or her status.

There are four basic temperament and personality types — DOERS, KEEPERS, THINKERS, and DREAMERS. These types are distributed throughout the band at roughly forty percent Doers, forty percent Keepers, ten percent Thinkers and ten percent Dreamers. Each of the types is a specialist in his band, providing his skills to keep the band efficient and running smoothly.

Finally, we are bullied by our programmed emotions. We have little control of our mental processes. We can have every intention of working on a logical task, but if a sexual opportunity presents itself, a status enhancement presents itself, or a fight breaks out, we are off. We can't say no to our emotions.

If our emotions are excited to a high pitch, we can explode into a supercharged, altered consciousness with a tunnel focus. We will give our all in hate and rage if our belief system or our loved ones are threatened. We are able to steer our emotional life but not drive it with any precision. We are never in complete control.

OUR MAJOR MOTIVATORS

N OW THAT WE HAVE an outside perspective on the social interactions of our band — the background that produced our programming — it is time to take a closer look at my list of a dozen of the major players in our programmed emotional and motivational makeup — FEAR, STATUS, US AND THEM, RELIGION, SEX, FAITH, DENIAL, VIOLENCE, HATE AND VENGEANCE, ICONS, and LOVE. They are my list of the engines that produce the most human energy — the most excitement and motivation. While our personal set of programmed abilities and temperament gives us our differing preferences in social interactions, food, clothing, music, humor, and art, we all share much the same reactions to fear, status, us and them, religion, sex, faith, denial, violence, hate and vengeance, icons, and love. These are our deep core boilerplate motivators that we all have in common.

We are not fountains of inexhaustible energy. A human is worth about three minutes of all-out effort and we are done for (boxing rounds are three minutes in duration). We are in constant danger of running out of gas. In the wild, running out of gas was a life and death matter. We have a programmed ancient energy conservation program. Our energy thermostat is on economy until we are motivated. Our mind is like a snow globe. Shake it up and it whirls around in wondrous activity. Let it sit and it settles into a quiet, restful sleep.

Evidence of this is everywhere. People endlessly circle parking lots so they will not have to walk an extra hundred feet. Paths are worn across lawns because to stay on the walkway would cost more steps. We are programmed to not spend any energy unless we are motivated to. We are like the lions in all those nature films on TV, aimlessly lolling about in the shade. An adult lion spends about four hours a day on its feet and it takes twenty hours of rest to support those four hours of hunting. And so it is with us — we are essentially on energy-saving hold until our senses (our monitoring systems) perceive something that motivates us, captures our attention, and triggers our energy release — FEAR, STATUS, US AND THEM, RELIGION, SEX, FAITH, DENIAL, VIOLENCE, HATE AND VENGEANCE, ICONS, and LOVE.

Fear

Fear is our number one motivator. Without fear, few animals would last long in the wild. Over the millions of years that our programming was written, there was a lot to be afraid of. There were numerous big predators that were on the constant lookout for prey just like us. We were essentially one-hundred-plus pounds of slow tasty protein with no natural defensive weapons. This is where our fight-or-flight programming came from. In our early days it was mostly flight or freeze (we didn't have the natural tools to fight, so our best chance to survive was to freeze). Once we got going on the manufacture of weapons, we were able to turn the tables on our natural adversaries and get into the fight business.

The bad guys — we are all afraid of the bad guys. The only animals that now pose a threat to humans are other humans. The entertainment business runs on fear. In literature, movies, TV, and video games, the stock in trade is fear. The fear of personal injury, natural disasters, monster mythic animals, bad guys, losing love, losing status, and losing life. We are fear junkies. There are over a thousand new super roller coasters that were built in the last decade. We will gladly pay a stiff fee to get seriously terrified. Fear is our strongest excitement trigger — our greatest energy release hit.

While fear is used extensively by the media to get us high, there is a strong downside to fear. A constant dose of fear is toxic — damaging to our nervous system, our self-confidence, and our sense of well-being. An ongoing dose of fear can lead to depression and disorientation. Combat fatigue (the thousand yard stare), if experienced too long, can lead to mental disability. Today, terrorism is the weapon of choice for the disenfranchised. We are all afraid and as yet have not found a way to control terrorism, which in turn compounds our fear. So fear is at once our strongest stimulant and our debilitating dread. Fear rules our lives until we can gain control — then status steps up to run the show.

Status

EVERY VIABLE HUMAN BEING IS CONCERNED ABOUT HIS OR HER STATUS. Mother Theresa was concerned about her status with God. Status is our strongest social motivator. Status is our handle on life, our coordinates on the map, and the underlying structure that supports our social life. The yearning of the human soul is to be accepted and revered by our peers. Without status we have no direction and no place in the scheme of things. Status is the end all and be all of the communal human life.

Everyone's daydreams are about winning a big chunk of status. The adolescent boy shooting hoops in his backyard can be heard impersonating a sports announcer, "Five seconds left! The championship is on the line! The home team is two points behind! Bobby has the ball! He breaks free but he is well behind the three-point line! He shoots! It's good! The crowd goes wild!! Grown men dream of being the star quarterback who wins the super bowl, winning golf championships, being rich and powerful, being dominant. Women dream of being the belle of the ball, being beautiful, being rich, being brilliant, being in control. We all lust after status. We can never get enough.

We have a fear of losing what status we have gained. Men will not ask for directions — they can't maintain their status, power, and control while asking for help from another. Women are reluctant to share their actual age — youth and beauty are important components of the feminine status base.

Social experiments have discovered that if someone is talking to another in a noisy group and their name is mentioned softly from far across the room, they will not only hear it but they will suspend the conversation they are in and listen only to that soft voice in the distance. We are so concerned about our status — what others are saying about us — that we can hear nothing else.

Status is a combination of who your parents are and what you contribute to the band. In a band of one hundred and fifty, status is carved in stone. Each individual knows exactly what the status of every other member of the band is. No one can fool anyone. They all know each other intimately — every mistake, every indiscretion, every strength, and every weakness. There is no place to hide; there is no room for deception. "Your status" has been defined as "other's reaction to you." The other band members who observe and interact with you give you your place in the pecking order. This makes for a stable society — everyone knows where he or she stands. That's the way our software jelled over millions of years. Now it is hard-wired.

Now, seemingly overnight, we live in a massive society of strangers — countless unknown faces that seldom register our existence. Yes, today we still have family and friends (our band of a hundred plus), but they are usually scattered all over. We seldom see them for more than a couple of hours at a time. Our once insular community that gave us our status and identity is gone and with it our automatic status rating. What are we to do? Most of us make up our status with equal parts wishful thinking, status icons (cars, living quarters, clothes), and a sprinkling of white lies. We fashion just as positive a story as we can about ourselves and still keep a straight face.

We are so used to people exaggerating their own status that one humorist noted, "One is now considered arrogant if he fails to promote himself." Most everyone you meet hints at having rich and powerful friends and relatives. Most men have athletic stories of their youth that tend to be unbelievable. Women often mention their teen "modeling days." Not all status seeking is in the "big house-car-money" category. There are an infinite number of status ladders and everyone is on one. The intellectual crowd competes for status with published papers, advanced degrees, and a Subaru. People also stake their status on their knowledge of art, music, cars, classic movies, etc. Still others pursue a "committed rebel" status, based on how strongly they oppose establishment forms of status. The examples are endless.

What are we doing? Why do we compromise our self-respect to appear to be someone we really are not? Because it works. Humans cannot function without status. We are programmed to relate to others through our status. We all believe that we should have more status (looks and a whole lot of money). We feel we are falling behind and need to catch up. Without status we are ships without rudders. In an ancient band situation, this couldn't happen. We would know the status of everyone involved. In our modern society, status is up for grabs. Our status is how much youth, beauty, knowledge, goods, money, power, and social connections we can project.

Status and sex are so intertwined in the human drama that they cannot be considered separately. For males, status is the road to alpha females. For females status and power is her programmed preference in mating — the best genes to get the strongest offspring. Status is the path to security for her young and a better quality of life for her family.

Status and power are the same in the human drama. You can almost always substitute one word for the other while discussing social dynamics and no one will be the wiser. We can also safely say that status has everything to do with a human animal's quality of life. We are primates and primates are socially organized according to each member's status within the troop. The higher the status, the better the food, the living conditions, the mating opportunities, and the individual's sense of well-being.

Most everyone lives in a house and neighborhood just beyond their means — STATUS. Most everyone drives a car they can't really afford — STATUS. Most everyone dresses in clothes of the "in group" and attend social functions where they vie for STATUS.

The same house that goes for a million dollars in a status neighborhood can be had for half that in a less desirable zip code (the three most important things about a house that's for sale are location, location, and location — read, status, status, and status). We are programmed to play status games. There was nothing in our ancient experiences in nature to prepare us to live in groups of thousands, let alone millions. We are small-troop animals adrift in a sea of our own kind. Our programming insists we compete for status, but in groups of tens of thousands we feel frustrated.

Our programming assumes that we will, at some time in our life, be the first, second, or third best at something in our world — our band. Say in a band of one hundred, there would be about fifty males and fifty females. Of those fifty, twenty would be too young and ten would be too old, leaving twenty to compete against. With a lot of effort and luck, it was possible for most band members to achieve status as a hunter, weapons maker, storyteller, teacher, healer, etc. Today, we know this as "getting on the podium" — coming in first, second, or third. Today, competing against thousands and establishing a sound status is a daunting task.

As Stone Age humans, status served as a means of keeping our band organized, cohesive, and well bred. It was important to our survival. Now, outside of nature's framework, bolstering our status is a programmed imperative that has us frantically competing against each other to acquire strong social connections, information, power, wealth, and status symbols. Since status, wealth, and power are all relative concepts, we are trying to play an impossible game. No matter how much status-wealth-power we achieve, there will always be someone with more. The energy we have generated playing this impossible game has propelled us from a hunter-gatherer animal to interplanetary traveler.

If you are to have a high status rating, as our programming insists you have, others must have a lower status rating. We must have losers to have winners — our subjective programming demands it. Again, we need to see that we can't judge or change the way we are programmed. We must play the genetic cards we are dealt. Status is the glue that cements us to our animal emotions.

We could have peace and plenty for all if we were logically driven — if we were able to live objective lives. The fact of the matter is that we are STATUS driven. We are genetically programmed to live subjective status-driven lives. We will fight to be one up on the other in order to feel superior — to get that status rush. Without the emotional feeling of above-average status, we can't generate enough self-confidence to attain a sense of well-being. We must have respect. We need to be honored and deferred to in our band. We must be winners.

We are so engrossed in playing our status games that we are compromising our life support system — our biosphere. We have the material, the know-how, and resources to peacefully feed, clothe, house, and educate every human on earth; all the things we believe we want for the human species. Because our programming locks us into playing competitive status games, we have a war-torn world, with two-thirds of the population living in crushing poverty while the other one-third is damaging the biosphere with its excesses.

Us and Them

US AND THEM is a function of the need of ancient hunter-gatherer bands to control their home hunting grounds — their food supply. Without this control, everyone's life was in danger. This concept is a deep one, going way back to basic animal software: defense of band and territory. All humans that were not members of your band had to be excluded from your territory — US AND THEM. Anyone you didn't know to be a member of your band was a threat. Where there was one stranger, there was the possibility of many — a raid — a major threat to all.

We are programmed to win, to confidently and aggressively take care of our own and defend them from outside dangers. Our programming automatically divides the world into US AND THEM. Our programming gives US the moral high ground and THEM no right to exist. We (our band) are always right. They (the other band) are always wrong no matter what the facts say.

The BBC produced what they thought was a nonpartisan documentary (an outside perspective) on the Palestinian-Israeli conflict. Before broadcasting the finished project, they showed it to officials of both governments. After viewing the documentary, the Palestinian officials proclaimed it blatantly pro-Israeli, while the Israeli officials denounced it as decidedly anti-Israeli and pro-Palestinian. When it comes to US AND THEM, we are programmed to accept a lopsided view of events — US as the no-fault good guys and THEM as the scum of the earth. That's the heart of US AND THEM. We are all right — they are all wrong.

We are programmed to attack anyone we don't know or isn't just like us. Ancient band territories usually could only just sustain the local band. The presence of others could mean starvation. In the present-day cities of hundreds of thousands of others, US AND THEM is a hard program to endure. We are in a constant state of arousal and anxiety. We are in a sea of strangers of differing color, dress, manner-isms, and religions. We either withdraw inwardly or affect an aggressive-dismissive attitude. The good news is that in cities like New York, with hundreds of ethnic groups inter-acting for over a hundred years, US AND THEM is slowly melting. Yet even in New York, US AND THEM can break out in violence in an instant — it is how we are programmed.

US AND THEM is elastic. Say two families vying for status in a community have an US AND THEM relationship. They compete for the same status and despise each other. Then a threat to the community, a flood, or a wildfire occurs. The two families are suddenly fighting side-by-side to save the community. If two communities have an US AND THEM relationship and the home nation of the communities is attacked, then the two communities drop their differences to come to the aid of their country. When we perceive a threat from the outside, we stop our intramural conflicts so we can fight the bigger fight.

Conflict is the mother of energy. With no conflict, we are programmed to snooze. With conflict, we are at once motivated and energized. It has been estimated that the motivation and energy generated by the pure US AND THEM of the Second World War caused mankind to achieve hundreds of years of technological advances in less than a decade.

US AND THEM is our constant motivator. If there isn't conflict in a group, there soon will be. Remember, status is the goal of every person. We compete for status even when we are not aware of it. We compete for and promote status for our family, our community, our ethnic group, our religion, our nation, and ourselves. When we combine status competition with an US AND THEM base, we generally get the possibility of war.

Fortunately, all US AND THEM does not have to lead to war. We can simulate US AND THEM combat and still get the energy rush. A benign example of US AND THEM is organized sports — the emotional equivalent of war. Most everyone has some sport they follow. We feel we know the players on our chosen team. We feel their pain when they lose and their joy when they win. Sports are an enactment of our band warfare programming. Our band's war party doing battle against their war party — US AND THEM.

"Sport is where an entire life can be compressed into a few hours, where the emotions of a lifetime can be felt on an acre or two of ground, where a person can suffer and die and rise again on six miles of trails through a New York City park. Sport is a theater where sinner can turn saint and a common man become an uncommon hero, where the past and future can fuse with the present. Sport is singularly able to give us peak experiences where we feel completely one with the world and transcend all conflicts as we finally become our own potential."

— George A. Sheehan

Video games present a new way to exercise our US AND THEM programming. We can participate in most any war we want. We can kill enemy soldiers, tanks, fighter planes, and feel the rush of victory without getting out of our chair.

The dark side of US AND THEM is all too familiar; segregation, ethnic cleansing, apartheid, war, bigotry — Black vs. White, Catholic vs. Protestant, Jew vs. Muslim, French vs. German, and on and on to Ford/Chevy, New York/Los Angeles — US AND THEM. The list is endless. We really can't help ourselves. We are programmed to automatically divide the world into US AND THEM.

Religion

Religion has been our rock, the handle we hang onto to fend off the uncertainties of life. For fifty thousand years, our Stone Age forbears knew their world only through spirits, Gods, ghosts, and apparitions. They had no science. They were in a beautiful hostile world that they had no way to understand the workings of except through their creative imaginations. We have this wonderful brain that not only thinks about everything it perceives, but also must know the why. Without knowing the whys of life, we are off-balance — mentally incomplete. In our Stone Age days we had many "WHYS?" Why did it thunder and lightning? Why are there rainbows? Why are there stars in the sky? Why are there four seasons? When you can't figure out why something is occurring; you can't rest until you know. You toss and turn and can't get to sleep. We must know why.

Our Gods have been providing us with answers to the questions we couldn't answer for thousands of generations. We relied on our Gods for so long that the supernatural has become a permanent part of our genetic programming — our operating software. We all are programmed to believe in the supernatural. Our brains have been marinating in and depending on the supernatural for our entire time on earth. Like all human attributes, there is a descriptive bell curve for our belief in the supernatural. On one side of the curve is the religious fanatic and on the other you have the mildly superstitious. The middle of the curve is the bulk of the believers. Even the most outspoken atheist has a bit of the supernatural in his belief system.

Everyone is superstitious. Everyone has a lucky pair of golf socks, a talisman, or a set of lucky numbers. We are all believers in the supernatural — it is only in the matter of degree that we differ. In America, thirteen is considered an unlucky number. High rises have no thirteenth floor and on Friday the thirteenth people tend not to fly or take long car trips. In Australia, the number thirteen is lucky — they sell the most lottery tickets on the thirteenth of each month. There is little rhyme or reason to our supernatural beliefs.

For over ninety-nine percent of the time we have been humans, we had no explanation for the puzzling happenings in the world around us except through the supernatural. We had no science. Our big brains are "find-the-answer" machines. With no written word, no tools to measure, no time to ponder the substance and meaning of all we observed, we turned to magic for the answers. Only our Gods and spirits could explain the world we lived in. We depended on the supernatural for fifty thousand years. The supernatural is now a permanent part of our programming. We start our children on the supernatural early in life with stories of Santa Claus, the Easter Bunny, and the Tooth Fairy, then on to Harry Potter and Shrek.

Our religions are ready-made belief systems that satisfy our genetic inclination toward the supernatural. Through our upbringing and socialization, we usually absorb the teachings of the religion of our ethnic group. Our religions give us our social rules, our life rituals, and the comforting belief that we are not alone. We subjectively believe we are being looked after by an all-powerful force. This doesn't make much sense logically. Emotionally, subjectively, and genetically, it fits like a glove. It is what we are programmed to do.

> "The mind will always create morality, religion, and mythology and empower them with emotional force. When blind ideologies and religious beliefs are stripped away, others are quickly manufactured as replacements. If the cerebral cortex is rigidly trained in the techniques of critical analysis and packed with tested information, it will reorder all that into some form of morality, religion, and mythology. If the mind is instructed that its pararational activity cannot be combined with the rational, it will divide itself into two compartments so that both activities can continue to flourish side by side."
>
> — *E.O. Wilson*

Every human society ever studied has had an elaborate set of religious beliefs. Religion is defined as: "The expression of man's belief in, and reverence for, a superhuman power recognized as the creator and governor of the universe." We have a problem-solving mind that must know. We need our mental balance. In our Stone Age past we couldn't afford the time, energy, and frustration of pondering the unknowable whys of life. We were too busy trying to stay alive. To free ourselves from this dilemma, we imagined an all-powerful set of Gods that were at once the creator of all we behold, our fatherly support system, and our ever-watchful disciplinarian. We created our creator.

It seems that over half the human population is programmed to accept God with complete faith. Their belief system is dominated by religious teachings. They cannot use logical deduction on questions that have already been answered by their faith. Abortion, prayer in school, birth control, same-sex marriage, and many other matters of life are not up for discussion. In their world of faith, denial of logic gives them a set of never-changing rules and guidelines. They do not have to face an ever-changing world. They are safe and secure in the hands of God.

To people who have a strong genetic predisposition to religious faith, there is the possibility of complete immersion in Church dogma. Once they have forsaken the imperfect world and given themselves to their God, a great burden is lifted. They no longer need to struggle with life. They completely accept the teachings and power of their faith. God will guide them. God will protect them. God will accept and love them. They are free.

The following is a selection of quotes from Andrew Sullivan's book *The Conservative Soul*:

> "Something about the visit to the U.N. by Iranian president Mahmoud Ahmadinejad refuses to leave my mind. It wasn't his obvious intention to pursue nuclear technology and weaponry. It wasn't his denial of the Holocaust or even his eager anticipation of Armageddon. It was something else entirely. It was his smile. In every interview, confronting every loaded question, his eyes seemed calm, his expression at ease, and his face at peace.
>
> So let me submit that he is smiling and serene not because he is crazy. He is smiling gently because for him, the most perplexing and troubling questions we all face every day have already been answered. He has placed his trust in the arms of God. Just

because it isn't the God that many of us believe in does not detract from the sincerity or power of his faith. It is a faith that is real, all too real — gripping billions across the Muslim world in a new wave of fervor and fanaticism.

That sense of certainty has even entered the democratic politics in the U.S. We have, after all, a proudly born-again president. Religious certainty surely cannot be disentangled from George W. Bush's utter conviction that he has made no mistakes in Iraq. "My faith frees me," the president once wrote. "Frees me to make the decisions that others might not like. Frees me to enjoy life and not worry about what comes next."

The dark side of religion is all too familiar in today's world. We are programmed to accept a religion as the basis of our belief system. If others do not share our religious dogma, we will fight the infidel (the non-believer). If others insist that their religion is superior or dare to ridicule our religious beliefs, we go ballistic. Something snaps. We can't handle the possibility that there is nothing to our strongly held beliefs. Our religions are often the framework that holds up our whole life. If an outsider depreciates or doubts our religious beliefs, our life will have no meaning. We must destroy the blasphemy to get our lives back.

Ironically, the major religions feature much the same message. Love thy neighbor, do unto others as you would have them do unto you, and peace on earth. Yet religious wars are the cruelest, hardest fought, and the least likely to ever be resolved. As recent history can attest, religious wars can become hell on earth.

Sex

This is a big one. Sex can be claimed as the point of life as in — *the point of life is more life.* Outside of survival and status, sex is our predominant motivation. Unlike other animals that have a protracted rutting season, humans are sexually active year round. It has been claimed that healthy males have a sexual thought every fifteen seconds. That may be a bit over the top, but the point is made. Through our programming we are obsessed with sex.

Our programmed responses to sexual stimulation are so strong that to engage in sex with another is to go into an altered state of consciousness. Our heart rate skyrockets, our focus narrows, the world is shut out, we are possessed by primal powers, and can achieve a supercharged rush that we return for again and again. It is believed that our preoccupation with sex was natural selection's answer to the question: How do you raise a human baby that requires at least a decade of extensive nurturing before it can survive on its own? Sex. The lure of ongoing sexual satisfaction with the mother of a man's children kept the father around, protective and supportive of the mother and the child.

Men are sexually attracted to women by their looks and women are sexually attracted to men by their power. Again, this isn't right or wrong, fair or unfair — it is the way we are programmed.

Let's take it one at a time. Men are sexually attracted to women for their looks. The looks that men are programmed to respond to are youth and beauty — the best chance to get the best genes into the next generation. That youthful, budding, just-about-to-blossom look of women's late teens and early twenties — men can't help themselves. In the ancient band of about one hundred, this programming produced the best possible gene combinations to produce the strongest, healthiest offspring — the alpha males competing for mating rights with the alpha females.

In our modern world, this programming causes all sorts of drama. Men can't help it. It's one of the strongest parts of their programming. It drives them crazy. In the best-case scenario, the man at an early age connects with Miss Right, falls in love; they reproduce and live happily ever after.

More often, men find themselves generally satisfied with their married partner but can't shake the lure of other women. Their programming demands that they spread their seed around. They can use self-discipline and religious support, but over several years, their overpowering programmed demands will have their way. That alpha female pull — the need to become sexually engaged with a beautiful young woman — is irresistible.

Men are so strongly programmed to respond to alpha female visual contours that they can't see, hear, or understand anything but their desire. This understandably infuriates older women, mystifies young women, and creates most of life's truly awkward moments. Divorce courts, police blotters, newspapers, novels, and movies are energized with the drama of inappropriate sexual activity.

Yes, women are also attracted to men by their looks. But it is the status power that is the clincher for women (Woody Allen and Henry Kissinger were once voted the sexiest men in America). We see this dynamic every day; an older man of indifferent looks but obvious wealth, with a beautiful young woman. Or the beautiful young woman with an aggressive athlete, political leader, doctor, military officer, actor, gangster, or brooding malcontent — any man that has social, financial, political, or physical power (better yet all four). Women can't help it. It is the way they are wired.

If a man has status and power it means that he is the best breeding stock, the best at controlling his environment, the best at protecting and providing for his offspring — in other words, the fittest. Most of us have known beautiful, charming, intelligent women who are with real jerks. Humorless, crude, it doesn't matter as long as the man has power, she can't help herself. That is why men buy cars they can't afford, pump iron, brag and cheat, fight and posture — all to project a sense of power to attract the alpha girl.

Here again we have a situation of once-appropriate software going all goofy in our new social environment. In a band of one hundred and fifty people it was less complicated — say fifty are children, twenty are too old, and sixty are already paired off. That leaves ten possibilities at most for mating partners. Since you would be closely related to about five others, you would have about five choices for a mate — that's it. Mating was relatively simple.

Today we live in a world of unlimited mating possibilities. With modern contraception, transportation, and communication, sex is omnipresent. Even with legal marriages, families with children, and religious prohibitions, the pressures of our software and opposite sex availability are proving to be too much. A situation that was usually settled by our late teens in the Stone Age band is now a life-long competitive struggle, with everyone looking over each other's shoulders for a better mate.

I don't think this is all terrible. Modern life may be filled with anxiety, but it is also more exciting, productive, and multi-faceted than ever before in our history. Our lives as hunter-gatherers may have been in accordance with nature and ecologically sound, but we lived a brutal short life in the bush and were not necessarily happy and fulfilled while we were doing it. Life was hard. I believe these to be the best of times.

Again, our mating process isn't right or wrong, it is how we are programmed. Fifty percent of married men have extramarital sex. It has been found that thirty percent of the babies born in hospitals were not fathered by the man recorded on the birth certificate. This all sounds terrible to our denial and religious beliefs system, but it is how we are programmed to behave — to seek alpha sex regardless of the possible social costs.

Faith

FAITH: Belief that does not rest on logical proof or material evidence.

> "Today, as always before, the mind cannot comprehend the meaning of the collision between irresistible scientific materialism and immovable religious faith. We try to cope through a step-by-step pragmatism. Our schizophrenic societies progress by knowledge but survive on inspiration derived from the very beliefs which that knowledge erodes."
>
> — *E.O. Wilson*

Faith is our rock with a handle. Unless we have a fixed reference point from which we can expand, we are in a constant state of energy-draining confusion. The rules will keep changing and we will not know where we are. We have faith in our religions, our family, our nation, and even our sports teams. A never-changing reference point in our lives grounds us.

> "Treat the other man's faith gently; it is all he has to believe with. His mind was created for his own thoughts, not yours or mine."
>
> — *Henry S. Haskins*

If a band of Stone Age humans didn't completely believe in themselves, they were doomed. Nature favors the confident and aggressive. The people and bands that believed in themselves survived. So, through Darwinian pressure, faith became a part of our programming.

"All the strength and force of man comes from his faith in things unseen. He who believes is strong; he who doubts is weak. Strong convictions precede great actions." — *J.F. Clarke*

Faith plays a strong role in making us believe that our perspective, our point of view, is THE perspective. We have all witnessed a political or religious argument where both sides keep repeating their point of view and not listening to a word of the other. Through faith they both know that they are right and the other is wrong. Our band has its status — its belief system — on the line and we can't give an inch. If our belief system is proven wrong, then we have no value, no viability, and no status. We have faith in our band's belief system and will fight to the death for it, no matter how flawed it is.

Denial

DENIAL: Refusal to grant the truth of a statement or allegation.

Denial is the censoring and withholding from ourselves any information that we cannot incorporate into our consciousness and still maintain our status and self-confidence. Denial is a kind of filter that blocks out information that could shake our faith or hurt our sense of status. Denial is a sort of secretary that throws out the mail and blocks calls that we can't handle — anything that could negatively impact our self-confidence and status.

Children give us insights on ourselves because they say it like it is. They haven't as yet learned any sophisticated social strategies. It just comes out as they feel it, as they are programmed. When a child of four spills his milk he says, "I didn't do it." That is pure human denial — I didn't do it. If it reflects badly on us — we didn't do it. It didn't happen on our shift. If more than one person is involved, it's their fault. Again, this isn't right or wrong or silly or childish, it is the way we are wired. We are wired to keep a positive, confident personal outlook, and if any information to the contrary shows up, we automatically deny it.

We can logically see that the filling in of wetlands is bad for the wildlife, but before we can entertain any thought of setting aside valuable land that could be developed for profit, denial steps in. It is like awaking from a dream — our head clears and we know intuitively that human use of the land is far more important. Let the ducks go somewhere else. We need more jobs, money, social power, and status.

We have faith in our preeminence and denial to stop any questions — our one-two punch that stops any self-reflection. That is our programming telling us we are the only beings of real importance. It is the same process that had us believing that the earth was the center of the universe. The same programming that has all those gonzo sports fans screaming, "We're number one — we're number one!"

Even after Galileo proved that the earth circled the sun, it was over one hundred years before his hypothesis was officially accepted as fact and another hundred years before the general public accepted it. Our programmed, deep-seated conviction that we are the dominant beings of the universe will not allow us to entertain any thoughts to the contrary. We are software-driven to reach the next status level and to never stop and consider anything other than our personal or group status. Faith and denial can't allow us any thoughts of vulnerability. If we keep worrying about wildlife, pollution, and population, we will never get that status we must have.

Together, faith and denial is the omnipresent set of blinders that keeps us from having to acknowledge any self-doubt or status loss. Faith and denial are the single biggest roadblocks to our achieving an outside perspective on ourselves — to logically understand our subjective programming. As soon as we start to get any insight into the programmed behaviors that are not all-together flattering, faith and denial cut in to nip them in the bud. In a phrase, WE CAN'T HANDLE THE TRUTH.

Violence

In nature, violence is the final decider — the final arbiter of status conflicts. We are programmed to threaten, posture, and negotiate for what we need. If all else fails we resort to violence. Nothing is quite as satisfying as smiting an evil-doer who is threatening our belief system.

Television shows and movies are excellent indicators of how people are programmed. Violence is what excites us, what we respond to, and what we are willing to pay for. Just look at the movie section of any newspaper — chain-saw murders, war action movies, medieval slash and stab, police shoot-outs, gang-bangs, car crashes, horror movies — end of the world mass destruction. This is who we are. When we go to the movies, we are really voting for what we want to experience the next time.

Destruction and violence are deeply woven into the fabric of our ancient programming. The lives we led in our hunter-gatherer days were forty times as violent as they are today (twenty percent died a violent death then vs. one-half a percent today). Violence was encoded into our programming during those millions of years when our lives depended on "kill or be killed." Today we seek outlets for all the violence we are programmed to perpetrate and endure.

We need our violence fix. Fear, sex, and violence are some of our most exciting programming modes. What we enjoy most is being as excited as we can get. That is what the movie and television writers and producers give us, all our energy triggers tripped at once — conflict, speed, sex, death, destruction, mayhem, blood, revenge, the kill, fear, and war — VIOLENCE.

74

Hate and Vengeance

HATE: To regard with extreme aversion; to detest.

Hate usually emerges from statements or actions that undermine a personal or group belief system. The only reason one person gets mad at a second person is that the second person isn't doing what the first person expects or wants him or her to do. What the first person invariably wants is for the other to respect him — to give him and his belief system approval, understanding, and status. The second person resists giving status and respect to another because he needs it himself. Emotional triggers are tripped and friction ensues. If the offensive act is strong enough, vengeance is contemplated.

VENGEANCE: The act or motive of punishing another in payment for a wrong or injury he has committed.

Vengeance is the acting out of hate. Terrorism is an expression of Islamic hate and vengeance. The World Trade Center was an act of hate and vengeance. The sectarian violence in Iraq is hate and vengeance. The whole Middle Eastern area is enveloped in hate and vengeance.

Vengeance is an amalgam of status loss, US AND THEM, and violence. We can't let a major status loss go unchallenged. We are wired to strike back. Our programming demands it. Our status, our religion's status, our nation's status cannot be allowed to suffer without retribution. If our self-esteem or our belief system has been attacked, we must even the score with great violence and fury.

Ethnic cleansing is an extreme example of vengeance: "These people are different from us and they have disrespected our belief system, our religion, our way of life, so they must all die." The Biblical saying, "an eye for an eye," is a call for restraint, a call for the offended party to restrict its vengeance to an equal response rather than killing everyone concerned. The tragedy of vengeance is that we don't stop at an equal response. We feel an urgent need to punish the offense so severely that the offenders will never even think of disrespecting us again — we will teach them a lesson they will never forget.

> "If you have committed iniquity, you must expect to suffer; for vengeance with its sacred light shines on you."
>
> — *Sophocles*

Icons

In our Stone Age past, we had speech but no writing system. We came to invest emotional content and status into items — a headdress for leadership, necklace for best hunter, cave paintings for hunting stories, and animal carvings for luck and courage. Icons were the only lasting record that Stone Age people could keep. Over thousands of generations, fertility, hunting, religious, and leadership icons unified the band and gave it status and meaning.

Belief in icons is deep and powerful. We take an object that has reference to an emotional occurrence and infuse it with meaning and magic. Example: in their dealings with the American Indians, the traders of the eighteenth and nineteenth centuries had great success trading steel knifes and hatchets for animal furs. They noticed that all the Indians had decorated shields made of animal hides. The traders had similar-sized shields made of sheet metal thinking they had a new best seller. The Indians would have none of it. Puzzled, the traders asked why the Indians wouldn't want the added protection of the stronger shields. The Indians replied that it was the painting of icons on their shields that protected them, not the shield itself.

And so it still is with us today. We have icons that protect us and give us power and status — Cadillac, Lexus,

BMW, Calvin Klein, Rolex, Armani, Prada — the list is endless. Nations, businesses, and sports teams have logos and flags as their icons.

Control of icons can bring instant status. A Picasso can bring tens of millions at auction, yet a perfect copy of the same painting is available for about a hundred dollars. Men spend twenty thousand dollars for a power watch when a better-performing watch costs about fifty dollars. My favorite is the people who spend millions for a baseball that was hit out of the park to establish a new record. The ball is worth four dollars at most, but our genetic programmed belief in and need for icons has many trying to out bid each other in the range of millions of dollars. From an outside perspective, this is madness. From a human programming perspective, the control of this status icon is a chunk of social power and magic that can turn an also-ran into a celebrity.

Love

I have put love last not because it is a lesser motivator, but because it is different. The other motivators cause an energy release that sharpens our focus and primes us for action. Love releases energy to soften. We become warm and fuzzy. We are inclusive and bond with the other and in the right set of circumstances, love is a prelude to sex.

"It is possible that a man can be so changed by love
as hardly to be recognized as the same person."
— *Terence*

Love is another state of being — a different emotional landscape. Our constant status seeking is suspended and we place our happiness in the happiness of another. We are motivated to create a world that supports and protects the object of our love. But if that love is threatened, we can also be motivated to fight for it.

"The greatest happiness of life is the conviction that we are loved, loved for ourselves, or rather loved in spite of ourselves."

— *Victor Hugo*

My list of emotional motivators — fear, status, US AND THEM, religion, sex, faith, denial, violence, hate and vengeance, icons, and love — are what I believe to be the backbone of our behavior, what makes us human. These motivators have us competing and fighting in our band, and our band competing and fighting in our community and nation. We are driven by this Darwinian struggle to survive, mate, and get our genes into the next generation. This is what we are programmed to do.

Unfortunately, we are so consumed by this programmed quest that we are running roughshod over our biosphere. We have unbalanced nature. We must learn to control the environmentally damaging acts of our emotional life. If we are to survive in the long run, we must keep our biosphere healthy and hospitable to our form of life. The Darwinian struggle to evolve as humans will be pointless if there is no world left to sustain us.

OUR MODERN LIVES

N OW LETS TAKE OUR STONE AGE programming and its
influence on our human behavior and apply it to our
modern lives. We will look at our modern life from an outside perspective. We will see how our programming affects
our every decision, either consciously or unconsciously,
and how those decisions are impacting our biosphere.

We can override our ancient programming by employ-
ing discipline through reasoning and logic, but it is much
like swimming upstream. The current always drags us back.
For example, people all over the world spend countless
billions of dollars on lottery tickets. The odds of winning
the big jackpot are around one in seven million. That is not
just a bad bet, it is throwing your money away. You would
have to play the lottery every week for a hundred thousand
years to have a statistical chance of winning.

Why would we do something so foolish? Because chance
taking and gambling are a strong part of our hunter-
gatherer programming — we really don't have much of a
choice. Another good example is male size and athletic

ability. We presently live in an economy where gender, size, strength, and speed of foot have little or nothing to do with success in business. Yet something like seventy percent of CEOs are males over six feet tall. Being a good athlete is more important in our society than being an intellectually-gifted person. We are still programmed to follow large male athletes just as we did twenty thousand years ago.

The background white noise of modern life is charged with status competition. Our ancient programmed need to earn status through our physical contribution to our band of about a hundred and fifty is still in flower. We give friends and family Christmas, weddings, birthday parties, dinner parties, and picnics. We help friends move and visit the sick. Within our band we still have acceptance and status through giving to our band. In our ancient hunter-gatherer days, as far as we knew, there were less than four hundred people in the whole world. There was US (our band) and THEM (the other bands in our area) and we are programmed to fight THEM.

If we could focus on our band and let the rest of the modern world go we would be content and fulfilled. We would be following our programming. We now have thousands to compete with for status in our local area and millions to compete with nationally. We are engaged in an impossible task. In a band, everyone had a good chance to have their day — being approved of and needed by giving to others. Status in the wider world has morphed from the old giving to everyone in the band, to today's competitively seeking as many social honors, as many material goods, and as much power as possible. What was once a programmed need to give has now become a need to own and control.

This sounds bad but is really only different. This new form of status has been channeled into a positive position in First World countries. The usual way to project status today is through the making and spending of money on status symbols. We accomplish this by working with and hiring others — fellow workers, lawyers, accountants, middle managers, architects, contractors, salesmen, et al. By the energetic pursuit of status through money and social position, we are creating jobs. The bulk of our modern First World life consists of the manufacture, sales, maintenance, and recycling of status symbols. Our need to project status is stimulating our economy, creating jobs and, by extension, still giving to others.

Status is the game we play. Status is the way to sex. Beauty is a form of status. Social power is status. Control of icons is status. Athletic ability is status. Scholastic achievement is status. Money is at once both power and status. Status is our constant subconscious goal.

We are pursuing relative status when we are not even aware of our actions. This is easiest to see in children. When a three-year-old goes to another child's birthday party, she is apt to burst into tears when the birthday child gets all the presents and they get none. Where is their present? Where is their attention? Where is their status? Children haven't learned any social tact yet. The same thing happens to adults, but they are a little subtler in the same situation. For example, when a friend gets a new car, you ask him if it is the same model that had a recall last year. Why did you say that? Because, with his new car, he had gone "one up" on you in the status game and you reflexively had to knock him down a bit. Our subconscious is always on the job, picking up status for us or subverting another's status. We are in an ongoing game of status one-ups-manship. A quote from Gore Vidal says it well, "When a friend of mine succeeds, I die a little."

What about all the religious good deeds and altruism? What about all the fund-raisers for flood victims? Yes, we do have a seemingly selfless altruistic streak and love of our fellow man. That too is part of our genetic programming. We feel a rush when we help others in distress, but status is still in the mix. Status holds the trump cards.

When you are giving to another, you are a status cut above the person you are helping. You feel great. You are a relative status winner. The person you help is at first grateful but is at the same time wounded by his loss of status and your gain. We appreciate help from others in a time of need, but once the crisis has passed we are apt to turn against our benefactors. We don't have the programming to be in a subservient position to anyone except our Gods.

Again, we are programmed to seek the highest status we can achieve in our band of peers. This is our life's work. If we can amass enough status through money, status symbols, giving, controlling, working, and creating, we get a rush of well-being, self-confidence, and access to sex. If we fail to generate enough status, we are viewed with pity or contempt. No one wants to hang out with a loser. This is another instance of tension being built into our programming. On the one hand we have altruism and compassion, and on the other hand our stronger emotional self needs to be one up on those around us. That is why charity events are so successful. We can at once see ourselves as giving and caring and also feel a boost in our status.

This is the human pattern — the human drama. We must have respect from others or we lose our self-esteem, status, and self-confidence. We see this all our lives — parents wanting respect from children; children wanting respect in the family; adults wanting respect on the job, in the community, and on the sports fields. The only way we can keep these constant interpersonal conflicts from getting out of control in our mega populations is through an agreed-upon set of laws administered by a large well-organized legal system and police force.

Law and Order

The first need of any modern society is an effective law enforcement system. Without law enforcement, our programming takes us straight back to our Stone Age band mode — gangs (bands of around one hundred and fifty) fighting among themselves for food, sex, status, and respect. The people of the ancient Stone Age bands lived lives that were forty times more violent than our lives are today. There was band cohesion but when push came to shove it was violence that was the final arbiter.

While studying a Stone Age band still living in New Guinea, anthropologists found that the most beautiful woman in the band was proud to report that her first husband had been murdered by her present husband so he could be with her. Every family in the study had multiple members who had died a violent death. The band fought ongoing battles with neighboring bands. This is the natural behavioral pattern of human animal bands. This was a winning strategy in our Stone Age days. Today in our global village of six billion, with high-tech weapons and our ancient US AND THEM programming, a potential mega-disaster is always looming.

In the United States law enforcement is taken for granted. The citizens are so used to an equitable, effective system of laws that they only see it when it breaks down. Even in a First World country, if any locale has a breakdown in law enforcement, due to a major weather event or a large-scale riot, looting, burning, and murder break out within twenty-four hours as a matter of course.

We are a Stone Age time-bomb just waiting to explode. Law is society's way of controlling our inner subjective animal so that we can organize ourselves in larger groups than our programmed one hundred and fifty. As soon as law enforcement breaks down, our US AND THEM takes over.

Ethnic friction, religious differences, tribal disagreements, and economic inequities come to a boil and anarchy rules. We have so many examples — Bosnia, Palestine, the Congo, Katrina, Iraq — the list is endless.

We don't realize how big and important an organization law enforcement is. Yes, there is the local police force, but there is also the FBI, CIA, Army, National Guard, Immigration, Coast Guard, Air Marshals, Sheriffs, Highway Patrol, security guards and so on. Then there are legislators, attorney generals, lawyers, judges, juries, jails, courthouses, juvenile detention halls, and an army of clerks.

Law enforcement is job #1 for any society. We are not designed to live with thousands of others. We have learned that we can't trust ourselves in large numbers. We must have a heavy lid on our animal programming or we self-destruct. Without law and order there is no chance for civilization.

Physical Appearance

We get the majority of our information and make our life's choices and judgments from the look of things. There have been many psychological experiments done to determine how important looks are to a human being. One researcher said, "to round it off to the nearest percentage point — one hundred percent."

In one experiment, a jury was convened and identical trials were conducted for the same crime. One defendant was a beautiful woman, the other a plain woman. The beautiful woman was let off with probation. The plain woman got jail time. So it goes throughout the history of human society. The beautiful people get the job, the date, the promotion, the best seats in a restaurant, and the most smiles on the street. We want to know beautiful people. We want to be seen with beautiful people. We want to be beautiful people. This isn't right or wrong, but it is the way we are programmed.

The truth of the matter is that beautiful people comprise about one percent of the population. A further ten percent can be called attractive. That leaves about ninety percent of us with a lot of work to do, and work we do. Women wear high heels (they really are not that tall and their legs are not that long). Women wear padded push-up bras. They wear designer clothes, eyeliner, mascara, powders, hairpieces, perfumes, etc. Now they also have cosmetic surgery of various kinds. The competition is killer.

The men are no better. They buy cars they can't afford, do weight-lifting, have hair loss treatments, and are now catching up with women in elective surgeries. Having sex is a programmed imperative. We select our sexual partners primarily by their looks and status. We can't help ourselves. Our programming makes us do it. The role of looks is too strong to measure. As they say in show business, "it is better to look good than to feel good." Fortunately, even though we are programmed to be obsessed with looks, research has found that plain people have just as strong loves and just as passionate sex lives as the beautiful people.

Belief Systems

Our belief system is the structure that supports our mental balance. Most people are unaware that they even have a belief system. We all feel that we know how the world works, that we know the score. We have been around the block. This intuitive understanding of reality is actually our belief system.

We all share the same physical reality, wear relatively the same clothes, watch the same type of entertainments, and eat the same sort of food. Therefore we share the same human reality. No we don't. Let's go back and revisit the four main personality types. Remember the DOERS (forty percent of the population), the KEEPERS (forty percent), the THINKERS (ten percent), and the DREAMERS (ten percent) — they all live in different worlds. Each of the types has its own belief system, its own perspective on the world.

The Doer's world is all action. Doers must be free to do what there is to do. They care little about politics or other people's sensitivities. Their sense of status is centered on being seen performing physical feats with style. They see the world as a stage and playground. They believe that everyone else does too.

The Keeper's world is all responsibility. Keepers must see that the time-honored plan is followed. They must organize themselves and everyone else. They are into rituals, rules, standards, shoulds, and musts. Their sense of status is centered on possessions, honors, degrees, titles, traditions, and money. They see the world as a complex organization that must be maintained, respected, and upheld. They know this to be a universal truth — the way life is.

The Thinker's world is logical. Thinkers are compelled to measure, understand, predict, and control. They care little for fashion or social convention. They seek their status through new skills and understanding. Their world is one of facts, figures, and percentages — this is the only real world to them.

The Dreamer's world is one of human interactions. To Dreamers, the understanding of self and others is reality — the constant quest for the meaning of life. They feel that the spiritual landscape is the only worthwhile reality.

Right there we have four very different concepts of reality — four different types of belief systems — four perspectives on the world. Then take into account that we are seldom a pure Doer, Keeper, Thinker, or Dreamer but instead our own blend of the types. This creates a staggering number of belief systems and an infinite number of perspectives on reality. Yes, our belief systems do have a lot in common, but when you get down to the details, everyone is as unique as a snowflake.

We are intuitively certain that our belief system is *the* belief system, *the* point of view, *the* real world. If something is not part of our belief system, to us it doesn't exist. We are sure that if others would only stop and think about it they would see that our belief system is the one true perspective on life. We don't question our belief system. We unconsciously and consciously try to change other's beliefs to our beliefs. Conversely, we refuse to accept other's perspective or other's way of life. People either speak to us with respect and understanding for our belief system or we can't hear them. Disrespect our belief system and a confrontation is likely to occur.

Let's take a deeper look at our belief system. Remember, a belief system has two parts — our genetic predispositions (our programmed personality traits) and our life experiences (our upbringing). Whether we are going to be an introvert or extrovert, aggressive or reticent, competitive or complacent, sensitive or insensitive, loving or cold, patient or impatient, controlling or a follower, humorous or literal, is decided at birth. Those are the genetic cards we are dealt. Those are areas where we will be different from other people in our community. We have no control over our genetic programming. It is in place at birth.

The second part, our upbringing and life experiences, is where we blend with our community. We bond with our group (our band) through our religious beliefs, our sense of right and wrong, our sense of fashion, art, music, and our ethnic, regional, religious, and national sets of rituals and loyalties. The two together — our genetically-given personality traits plus our life experiences — gives us our BELIEF SYSTEM.

Our belief system has some common denominators. There is a similar boilerplate that comes with every belief system. Our belief system not only contains our programmed personality traits, mixed with our life experiences, but also a common basic inner core — the life force of every belief system. This life force tells us that we and our community are important. We are needed. We have a unique worth and so does our family, religion, ethnic group, and country.

This life force is the engine that drives the Darwinian theory — stay alive and reproduce. In order to stay alive and reproduce, we must believe in our community and ourselves. We don't just believe our community is superior. We know we are superior through our genetic programming and through the use of our blinders — faith and denial.

As we grow from infancy to adulthood we have stages, windows of opportunity to learn to walk, to speak, to run, et al. It has been found that if a child doesn't learn to walk between the ages of one and five he will never be able to walk fluidly. There is a time for us to learn to walk — a time when our nervous system is aligned with our programming to produce a walking child. If that window isn't used, we can still learn to walk later but not as easily or as completely coordinated.

Most of us have heard of people who have spent a prolonged time in a foreign country with their small children. Their children learn the local language within a month or two and end up translating for their parents. Their children are not Einsteins. They are simply at that chronological sweet spot for learning language. Their whole mental makeup is concentrated on language acquisition. It is one of the stages of development we all go through — one of our rhythms of life. It is the way we are programmed.

The same type of process is in place for acquiring our belief system. From the time we can walk and talk, we are primed by our programmed life rhythms to absorb our band's way of life — our band's moral codes, social taboos, rituals, core beliefs, gods, and superstitions. Once we reach pubescence, our core belief system is pretty much locked in. Our genetic behavioral programming has merged with our life experiences and produced our belief system. Yes, our belief system can change after pubescence, but it is very rare. It takes a great mental trauma or an act of great discipline to do so. We will always have the imprint of our original belief system.

If you were born and raised as an American. You will have an American belief system. You will be American for life. Adults who immigrate to America will be Mexican, Iranian, Chinese, etc., for the rest of their lives. They will, from an American point of view, continue to wear some aspect of their goofy native costume, listen to strange music, and participate in weird customs and beliefs. They really don't have a choice. They already have their belief system. There isn't anything they can or want to do about it. Their children, through their new socialization, will probably be half their native culture and half American. Their children's children will more than likely be American.

The influence the current American belief system has on international politics is all too obvious. The Bush administration seems to believe that America has the only righteous society and holds all of the great truths. America will help those less fortunate if they accept America's obviously superior way of life. America will save others from their backward ways. No wonder America is less than popular in the court of world opinion.

The Bush administration is denying other nationalities their belief systems — their programmed need for national pride. They are essentially saying "Your history, your traditions, your dress code, your religions, your way of life is not worth doing. America is better than you." Even in the most enlightened circles, those are fighting words. If America is to get along in the international community, it must allow other people their pride, dignity, and status — their belief system.

Political Correctness

This all brings us back to US AND THEM. One set of traits gives life to another. Our belief system is going to clash with other belief systems by mere definition. If two different belief systems come in contact, each knowing that their view on life is the only righteous view, conflict becomes inevitable — US AND THEM. All humans are guilty of this sort of discrimination. We are programmed to discriminate — to fight any ethnic, religious, or social group that isn't part of our belief system.

People want to think that they are not discriminating against others. That they are enlightened citizens. That they embrace diversity. That is all denial. We all discriminate. We are programmed to discriminate. We can't help it. Life is a process of discrimination. The human condition is now an unnatural one. We are programmed as an insular small troop animal. Now that we are living in groups of millions, the best we can hope for is discrimination management — being politically correct.

We tend to groan at politically correct statements. Let's be honest. We are seldom honest in our every day conversations. When you see an aunt for the first time in a couple years, what you notice is that she looks older and heavier. You don't greet her with, "You look old and fat."

We use a type of politically correct code when we speak to each other. We are so anxious about our relative status that we take accurate statements about ourselves as put-downs. We can't handle the truth. We want support and approval. If we don't get support and approval from friends and relatives, we feel like we have been attacked.

If we spoke our minds in personal conversations with no tact (no political correctness), we would be perceived as constantly putting people down. We would really only be telling the truth as we see it, but our listeners would take it as an insult. We all must feel we have status. We are so sensitive of another's opinion of us that we cannot handle the truth. We must keep our status and self-confidence on a positive level. If we always spoke our minds, we would have no friends. No friends equals no status. No status equals no social life. No social life equals depression, despair, and mental instability.

The truth of the matter is that being politically correct is the answer. Without respecting the other's point of view, their belief system, and their need for personal status, meaningful conversation is impossible. The key to getting anyone to listen to your point of view is to preface your statement with at least three compliments to your listener's belief system. You must show your listener that you respect him or his only response will be aggressive or defensive. He or she will not be able to hear you. Our belief systems are that strong. Not acknowledging your listener as an equal, even if he doesn't share your belief system, will only result in resentment and name-calling. A modern human life is an ongoing public relations exercise. Lincoln said it well, "I destroy my enemies by making them my friends."

We hate being politically correct to those not in our band. Our instincts (our programming) tells us to destroy them. Kill the intruders. Everything will be fine as soon as we get rid of the outsiders. That is why we love sports so much. In our politically correct modern world, sports are the only time our animal instincts are completely un-tethered — let loose. We are in a band war and loving every minute of it. Our belief system against yours. It is what we are programmed to do. We identify with and feel we know the star players on our team. If our team is winning a close game, we get so emotionally involved that we can't stay in our seats. We uncontrollably jump and leap about, shout-ing encouragement to our team. We moan and hurl insults when the opposition team scores — kill the bums! Sports are ritualized Stone Age band warfare — the essence of Darwinian struggle compressed into a couple of hours.

If our team wins, we experience giddy elation, pride warms our being, and all is right with the world. If we lose, we are distraught but filled with determination to win the next war. We support our fallen team and heroes, knowing that they will rise again. Sports are the playing out of our programmed Darwinian struggle to survive, overcome, and dominate — "the thrill of victory and the agony of defeat." All of our emotional stops are pulled out. We are at once excited, motivated, energized, and emotionally invested in the moment — our favorite state of being.

The expression of our gut feelings of US AND THEM is keeping our world in constant conflict — white against black, immigrant against native, rich against poor. These blanket — US AND THEM — gut feelings are only true in our animal programmed heads. The truth of the matter is that people are all the same. Between all the races, there is less than one-thousandth of one percent difference in our DNA. We are all the same people with differing belief systems.

Example: The Vietnam war was a military and political blunder, yet the fact that a large percentage of American young people had to live, work, and fight together in an integrated Army did more for racial harmony than all the "let's-all-get-along" speeches ever given. Blacks ended up with White friends for life. Latinos developed strong friendships with Blacks. The American social landscape was changed forever. Young people experienced the fact that in spite of our gut feelings of US AND THEM, race really didn't matter. We are all the same people. If we interact with THEM long enough we come to see that they are really US.

The only thing that separates Israelis from Palestinians is their belief system. They are the same people. The same holds true for the Pakistanis and the Indians — the same people with different belief systems. This is the madness of our current world of religious and ethnic wars. The young men that are killing, torturing, and maiming each other are the same young men. If they were to meet on neutral grounds they would enjoy each other's company. They would joke and horse around, talk of beautiful women, kick a soccer ball around, and have a beer or two.

Unfortunately, our intuitive programmed emotions not only cloud our personal relations, but are as equally strong in our international relations. Nations exhibit the same traits as the ancient Stone Age bands. Just as a person refuses to be a slave to another, a nation cannot tolerate being dominated and occupied by another.

A nation cannot tolerate subjection to another. The examples are endless: the African and Asian colonies of European nations in the nineteenth century, England and Ireland, Israel and Palestine, the old Soviet Union and the eastern European countries, and so on.

We can understand the basic mechanisms of our emotional life and see that they were designed by and for our former animal mode of living. We can further see that at this point in our history, our programming has turned against us. We are upsetting nature's balance by following our programmed dictates without questioning their impact. We are slowly destroying our habitat. We have become self-destructive.

Again, our programming is not right or wrong, it just is what it is and will be the same for at least the next few thousand years. The upside of all this is that if we work with our programming we can eliminate its rough edges. The movies, TV, and video games are a benign outlet for all our programmed need for violence. Our minds can't distinguish between virtual violence and real violence. We can have our violence fix and avoid all the death, destruction and environmental damage.

Our Communal Life

We need to see how strongly our communal animal programming affects our actions and our understanding of others and ourselves. One human is nothing. It is only through others that we can exist or have meaning. Your self is defined as other's reaction to you. You have no self except in relation to others. We need the acknowledgment from others that our actions have been noted and approved of or disapproved of — ATTENTION. Attention to a human is like water to a plant. We all must have attention from others. This is easy to see in children, "Look mom, no hands!" "Watch this, dad!"

The only important thing in a human's life is other people. We depend on others to define who we are, to give us meaning, to give us an identity, and to give us status. An individual's life quest is to find a support group that approves of one's personality, character, temperament, and contribution. Since the point of all animal existence is to reproduce, and status is the arbiter of who has sex with whom, it follows that status is the number one job for humans. We are organized by status. The status component is so strong in the human makeup that our other programmed traits are but the mane and tail on our status horse.

To again summarize, we are intelligent, curious, and industrious communal animals driven by fear, status, and sex, and have been programmed by natural selection to live in the wild in bands of one hundred and fifty. That is who we are. Yes, we have the powers of deduction and logic, but our lives are run on supernatural beliefs and animal emotions. The one point that should be understood and underlined again and again is that beyond survival and reproduction, what makes the human animal run is the promise of an energetic positive rush when we compete for and win status.

The way we can restore our wounded biosphere is to understand and work with our programming. To do this we must get past our programmed faith and denial. Our faith has convinced us that our belief system is without fault. Our denial keeps us from acknowledging that we are even programmed, let alone from questioning our programming. We must develop an outside perspective. We must learn to understand, accept, and deal with our now-inappropriate animal programming. Again, we cannot change our programming. We have to do what our ancient programming tells us to do. We have no choice. But we can, with a little ingenuity, channel our programming into benign, even productive, patterns.

PART TWO

A MACRO SKETCH OF HISTORY

FROM THE STONE AGE PROGRAMMING paradigm presented in Part One, we will now be looking at how our programming generated our history. Our ancient programmed actions and reactions were produced by our surviving for millions of years in our animal mode of life. Our wonderful big brain, over time, gave us objective scientific discoveries — agriculture, herding, and metallurgy. These objective advances put our animal lives on tilt. Our post Stone Age history has been an awkward seesaw adjustment between our subjective one hundred and fifty-person hunter-gatherer programming and our new agrarian large populations. I hope the reader will be able to use the human animal programming model to get a new perspective on human motivations and actions — our history.

This will be a macro sketch of western civilization's history. The thread that this history follows is a fast-forward from the Egyptian civilization to the First World War, then a more detailed account of the last hundred years from an American perspective. All this will be viewed through our

Stone Age programming. The names and dates of people, wars, elections, rebellions, and assassinations will be treated as unimportant by-products of the real conflict. The real conflict is always a clash between two or more nations over their STATUS and BELIEF SYSTEMS.

Nations behave in much the same way as individuals. Nations exhibit the same set of programmed emotional motivators as individuals. Nations must have respect from other nations. Nations have an inner drive to establish international status. With international status and respect, a nation gets the positive energy of a proud and motivated population, preferred trade relations, free passage in international waters, and deference from other nations. Without status, a nation will eventually be overrun by its neighbors, divided up, and will cease to exist.

Nations, just as all living things, have a life span. Nations usually start off with much excitement and emotional energy. The people fight, bond, and work hard to establish the nation's status. Then over time, as the population adapts to the nation's successes, they no longer feel as strong an energy rush from our US AND THEM, status, and kill or be killed programming. They tire of all the cost, sacrifice, hard work, and misery of war. They want to knock off and have a little wine. At this point, there are always hungry, motivated, underdog nations with a frustrated status thirst, willing to risk all in a war. Human history is a chronicle of this never-ending cycle.

The threat of war is ever-present in international interactions. There have been multiple wars going on around the world throughout history. If two ethnic groups live in close proximity, they will be at war at some time in their history. If two nations are at peace with each other, it is usually because they have combined to fight a third.

In our Stone Age days, we were in constant band warfare with our neighbors. We carried this tradition over into our new large agrarian societies. All the maps of the world were drawn by the outcome of wars or the threat of war. War is like the supernatural — it is so deeply entrenched in our programming that we can't even see it. Again, violence is the final arbiter in nature. It isn't right or wrong — it is just the way life is programmed.

The people who say that war has never solved anything are deep in denial. War is actually mankind's most successful tradition. All boys play war (some girls too). Boys are programmed to practice war in their games — Knights of the Round Table, cowboys and Indians, cops and robbers, civil war, star wars, World War Two, commando, etc. Now they play war on their computers for hours on end. War is in our blood, in our dreams, and in our genes — in our programming.

Young men the world over rush to join their armies. Wars have always been horrific. When viewed from a logical outside perspective, they are the soul of stupidity. Large damage is done to the infrastructure of both societies and the best young men are killed on both sides of the conflict. When it is pointed out to them that being a soldier in a war greatly enhances the chance of their being killed , they all know (through their Stone Age programming) that others may die in the coming fight, but it won't be them. It seems that you can lead a man to slaughter, but you can't make him think.

Throughout history, the great thinkers have condemned war and called for its end. They were assuming that we have rational control over our emotions but the opposite is closer to the truth. Our emotions have the upper hand. Men have a genetic imperative to fight for their woman, family, band, ethnic group, religion, and nation. Through our Stone Age programming the making of a man from a boy is to prove oneself in battle — the journey of the hero. The conquering hero is the highest status position a man can achieve.

Prior to around fifteen thousand years ago, the world-wide human population remained at about ten million or less. We were hunter-gatherers living the life that natural selection crafted for us over millions of years. We were in groups of about one hundred fifty, living off the land, and fighting any other bands that tried to horn in on our hunting grounds. Life was natural. We were programmed to live the life we were leading. We were running on automatic; essentially living an animal life in nature.

Then we discovered agriculture and herding. The food supplies multiplied and so did our populations. We went from about ten million worldwide to hundreds of millions in a couple thousand years. Cities arose and we were now farmers or merchants instead of warrior hunters. We were living in groups of thousands rather than hundreds. Class stratification replaced our old egalitarian band societies.

We are not emotionally equipped to deal with thousands of others. We had to break down our new large populations into numbers we could cope with — one to two hundred at a time. The new social order became ruling class, merchants, craftsmen, and peasants. This new arrangement didn't fit our programming. We wanted to drop our plows, get away from all these disturbing strangers, and go back to hunting and gathering with our old egalitarian band. It was too late. There were too many people to feed. Hunting and gathering could not support our new numbers. We are still having a hard time adapting to this new way of life our big brains produced.

The Egyptians, blessed with the most fertile river land in the world, were the first in the Middle East to build an organized agrarian civilization large enough and strong enough to resist the bands and tribes of looting marauders along their borders. During periods of comparative safety and calm, the sciences made their first appearance. Mathematics, stone masonry, writing, and philosophy were conceived. For a couple of thousand years, the Egyptians were the only nation that successfully kept their large population down on the farm, organized, and effective. Warfare was constantly in the mix. The Egyptians were overrun by the Persians, the Greeks, the Macedonians; and the tribes of the south and west applied constant pressure. It would take a hundred years or so to reclaim their country, expel the invaders, and start the cycle all over again.

The Greeks watched, admired, copied, and eventually conquered the Egyptians. The science, stone architecture, philosophy, and political organization was all new and exciting to the Greeks, at the same time that it had become the "same old, same old" to the Egyptians. The Egyptian empire became so successful that its large population lost its collective us against them cohesive edge and started to break back down into the programmed human need to be in bands of one hundred fifty. The Greeks became the torchbearers of this new civilized and scientific national experiment. The international competition was heating up. The Romans were organizing and copying the Greek successes, eventually overrunning the Greeks.

The Roman Empire was the eventual beneficiary of all this new technology. Through their objective organizational skills, they created the first modern nation with an effective bureaucracy, monetary system, and road system. Their navy and, disciplined well-equipped, army was more than a match for the smash-and-grab tribes that surrounded them. For hundreds of years, the Romans fought and conquered other nations and tribes, bringing the new sciences with them. Eventually, the Romans conquered the entire known world.

During this time, the warrior religions of many gods were being challenged by the new agrarian religions. A single protective all-powerful God became the new movement — the Jewish, Christian, and later Islamic religions. The new one-God religions had a passive martyr theme — love thy neighbor, lets all get along, life is hell but we will be rewarded in heaven. Times were changing and we needed to adapt. It was hard to get people to stay on the land and grow the crops that would sustain the new cities. The new one-God religions made suffering and self-denial a virtue and the kill-or-be-killed warrior code a sin. As the new religions made converts of even the Roman Empire, the stage was set for international change.

Humans, programmed only for adversity, have trouble with success. The Roman Empire rotted from within. With no one left to conquer, they lost their momentum, purpose, and edge. Corruption, graft, excesses, and finally apathy left the Roman Empire soft and clumsy. Under adversity, we are cooperative, motivated, energized, and focused. With success, we become egotistic, greedy, complacent, and self-indulgent.

About eight hundred years ago, the Vikings and their ilk took our old violent programming on the road. They pillaged and raped their way through the known world. They simply took or destroyed what others had created. Then they gathered up their loot and went back home to rest up, only to go out and do it again. This was mankind being pulled back to its old programmed warrior mode. We have no programming for farming and herding. People were confused, overworked, and bored. They longed for their old roots and the way of life they were programmed to live. With no real political agenda, the raiders just petered out and were assimilated into the societies they worked so hard to destroy.

We have this ongoing inner conflict between the OBJECTIVE and the SUBJECTIVE. This conflict has been confusing mankind ever since we left our band way of life. We have millions of years of accumulated genetic programming to live subjective lives as hunter-gatherers in groups of one hundred plus. We have no programming to live organized objective lives in mass populations with time-tables, quotas, and class structures. We have an ongoing love-hate relationship with science. The body demands the subjective. The mind demands the objective. The more science we employ, the less room there is for our subjective animal programming. The objective sciences have given us all of our technological advances, political organization, mechanical power, food for the masses, great buildings, and transportation. But our subjective emotions give us our lives — all our joy, love, art, sex, victory, hate, and revenge.

As Europe entered the Middle Ages, a new political landscape was forming. Merchant city-states were the movers and shakers. A multiplicity of small principalities with their own armies dotted the map of Europe. Trade was the engine that drove the new economies and the Catholic church, through the new Holy Roman Empire, was the common thread that wove them together. The Church and the rich merchants commissioned new works of art and music. The time we know as the Renaissance had begun.

The Catholic church purged the land of the pagan religions the people had returned to in the Dark Ages. Witches were burned and inquisitions were staged. It was brutal but effective. All of Europe became Christian, and the Catholic pope was running the international show. The little city-states became rich trading powerhouses. The age of exploration was underway and Europe was on the move. As always, war was an ongoing theme, but they tended to be smaller in scale. Europe was slowly taking shape under royal families as they united the principalities into the nations we know today.

The Catholic church became the first multinational corporation in the world. With warrior popes wielding great power and wealth, the Church exercised power and influence across state and national boarders. All across Europe, the Church built cathedrals that wowed the public. The cathedrals had beautiful soaring stone architecture, stained glass windows, and a massive scale that impressed and captured the imaginations of the people. It is hard for us to understand the impact of those cathedrals on the people of Europe. Most people lived in mud huts and were desperately poor. The cathedrals were the Disneylands of the time. They had stained-glass light shows, status, beauty, power, authority and everyone was encouraged to belong. The Church established itself as the way to heaven. People were Catholics first, and French, Spanish, Italian, etc., second.

As with any human endeavor, the Catholic church soon had a breakaway group challenging its authority. The Protestant church was founded to get the Christian religion out of politics and power-brokering and back into the spiritual realm. Any human enterprise that establishes a power base will soon have adversaries. Conflict is the mother of human energy.

Machiavelli, at the beginning of the sixteenth century, understood the dynamics of our ancient human programming. In his advice to a young prince, he recommended that the prince's first act after taking control of his country should be to trump-up a war with his weakest neighbor. In one stroke, he would emotionally motivate and unite his people behind him by exploiting their programmed need to divide the world into US AND THEM. At the same time, he got his people fighting for their collective STATUS and pride rather than squabbling among themselves and fighting him and his administration. With the probable success against the weaker neighbor, the prince would be hailed as a great leader while appropriating more land and/or money in the peace negotiations. In international politics, as in personal relations, winning and status goes to the clever, the dynamic, the aggressive, the confident, and the strong.

With the advent of the new monarchies came an international competition for the status that was gained from trade with distant lands. Sailing ships became the new exciting technology and the race was on to trade with the exotic East. Silk, china, tea, and spices became the new status symbols for the rising merchant class. Holland, Portugal, Spain, and England became rivals for supremacy on the seas. US against THEM for international status and pride became the engine that drove the new European nations. The chase was on and the energy was high.

Through all the sailing ship trade competition, a search for a new and faster route to the east discovered a whole new world — the Americas. At the time of the discovery of the American continents, the indigenous populations, while great builders, astronomers, farmers and organizers, were hundreds of years behind the European countries in metallurgy and weaponry. The Spanish and Portuguese were the first to exploit the Americas by brutally destroying one middle American civilization after another in the search for gold. With them they brought European diseases that, over a couple of hundred years, decimated the native populations, leaving the two new continents essentially empty.

Fueled by the prospect of gold to finance their continental wars, the European nations rushed to colonize the new lands. First the Spanish and Portuguese, then the French and English, established colonies. The main theater of international status was being played out in European wars. The colonies were also status symbols for the European nations, but they proved to be expensive and hard to control. What they really needed was more money to prove their power in the main show — the status wars in Europe.

The English colonies became the largest and strongest group in the new North American lands. The English crown, always strapped for money, tried to tax the new colonies to pay for their ongoing wars. With the help of the French, the American colonies broke away from the English and established the United States of America.

In Europe, the Age of Enlightenment had dawned. The thinkers were embracing the new sciences. New discoveries were the result of controlled experiments. This was our large brain finally getting a chance to flex its objective muscle. The age of alchemy was coming to an end and science was on the ascendance. Intellectuals in Europe were questioning politics — why couldn't man get along? At the time, it was believed that one of the big problems was the old royal families and aristocracy that were entrenched but incompetent. If only mankind could start with a clean slate — no royal families, court politics, or ongoing status and trade wars. With the help of the new sciences, mankind could start anew and this time make it all work.

The intellectuals of France were so enamored with the idea of a new start that they talked the French government into financing the American Revolution (it certainly helped that the French were more than happy to give England a bit of grief). The exciting idea was that here was the perfect chance to see if a workable government, based on the ideas of the enlightenment philosophers, could be constructed in a new land. The goal was to form a government of equality, justice, and self-determination, without any international status conflicts or royal families to deal with. It would be a bold social experiment.

America got off to a rocky start. It took another war with England to establish America as a recognized independent nation. The experiment seemed to be working well — no rigid class structure to hold them back and an all but empty continent to exploit. A great era of energy, individualism, discovery, and innovation began.

It was also a time of great upheaval in Europe. The French revolution made the other nations of Europe nervous, tending to their home fires and leaving America to its own devices. The new French republic was in dire need of cash and sold their vast American colonial lands to the United States. The United States, in the next fifty years, spread across the whole North American continent. Taking the old Spanish lands to the west, in a lopsided war with Mexico, completed the task.

The American Civil War is an excellent example of human programming. The north was deep into the industrial revolution. Steam power, railroads, new inventions, steel mills, mass production, and lucrative international trade called for a strong central government. The south was agrarian, raising tobacco and cotton for foreign trade. The south wanted to retain slavery, states rights, and a weak central government with little or no taxes. The north was proud of being the objective future. The south was clinging to the subjective past. It was a triple programming hit — US AND THEM, objective vs. subjective, and free vs. slave. The energy generated by this conflict is still resonating today.

The Civil War is still celebrated today. There are re-enactments of battles with flags flying, period costumes, rifles, and cannons. There are state parks marking where battles were fought. There is a whole body of literature that chronicles every event of the war years. There are countless novels, movies, and plays that celebrate the romantic mood of the time. To this day we embrace the energy, the romance, and the grandeur of the American Civil War. This is our war programming, our US AND THEM programming, our programmed need for heroes and a large dose of DENIAL all rolled into one energetic extravaganza. That is our programmed romantic view of the American Civil War.

The objective truth of the American Civil War is so tragic that our imaginations can't really grasp the horror of it all. The Civil War was the first large-scale war fought with the new weapons of the industrial revolution — masses of artillery, repeating pistols and rifles, observation balloons, and railroads. The railroads made it possible to get a hundred thousand men to a battlefield, then supply them with ammunition, food, and replacements. The Civil War was the first time that tens of thousands of men were killed in a single battle on a routine basis. The carnage from the new firepower was on an unprecedented scale and the deaths from diseases, due to poor sanitation, outnumbered the battle deaths. Man had created hell on earth. A military historian wrote that the First World War would probably not have been fought if the European nations had sent observers to witness the death and destruction produced by modern weaponry.

After the Civil War, the United States got a tremendous economic boost from the immigration of millions of chance-taking adult Europeans. It takes a large community investment to raise a child to an adult. America got millions of adult workers without having to finance their rearing and training. The emotional explosion, as the immigrants realized their dream of owning land and being their own masters, energized the whole country for the next century.

The First World War, "the war to end all wars," was all human programming. It really wasn't necessary. It was primarily caused by a perceived lack of respect by the Germans, and a European perception that life had become too soft and self-indulgent. It is also interesting that the national personalities of the major combatants were roughly those of the DOER (America), KEEPER (England), THINKER (Germany), and DREAMER (France).

In the short War of 1870, the Germans defeated the French. The French sued for peace and for the next forty years Western Europe enjoyed peace and prosperity — "the belle epoch." France, especially Paris, was the envy of the world. France was the worldwide center of art, fashion, and philosophy. At the same time, England was very proud of itself, enjoying the fruits of the industrial revolution. It had become the profitable hardware store to the world.

Kaiser Wilhelm and the German people were feeling left out of the party. They should be getting more status and attention. After all, they beat the French in the last war. They should be the "cock of the walk." But no, they were thought of as good at the new sciences but other than that, they had a reputation for being serious and socially crude. The Germans couldn't get any international respect.

Concurrent with the German feeling of status inferiority was the old human programming problem of not being able to handle success with any aplomb. We are great at adversity but terrible at success. We adapt to our success and then expect more while doing less. At this point in European history, more was everywhere. The invention of the internal combustion engine, the car, the airplane, electricity, and modern chemistry had the world abuzz.

At the time, the social thinkers of Europe believed that this prosperity and all the new toys had gone too far. Too much was changing too fast. Women were parading around Paris in obscenely expensive clothes. Men were overly proud of themselves and soft. It was subjectively felt that a "good war" would straighten all this out — it always had in the past. All the men would go forth, exercise their programmed need to be warriors, and get their manhood back. The women would have to keep the home fires burning and get a sense of purpose back in their lives.

Europe was primed for war. An elaborate web of alliances had the major powers obliged to come to the aid of other nations if they should be attacked by a third. The inevitable spark set off the powder keg. When war was declared, the church bells rang in London and people danced in the streets. They were in complete denial. It was universally felt that the war, having started in August, would be over by Christmas and they would all be better off for it. As we know, it wasn't over until four years later and no one in Europe was better off.

The two sides fell into trench warfare. Massive long-range artillery duels and mass frontal attacks left over a million dead in one campaign. The invention of the machine gun made a quantum leap in firepower. The war fell into a deadly stalemate, with the two sides rotting in their trenches looking at each other across a shell-pocked no-mans-land. A whole generation of young men died under the worst possible conditions. The trenches had standing water most of the time, giving the men trench foot. The no-mans-land was the target of thousands of artillery pieces during attacks. There were so many exploding shells that the earth was turned over, and to this day, human bones are found up to twenty feet deep in these old battlefields. There were so many dead that rats, feeding on the corpses, became the size of small dogs. Add to this the use of poison gas, the starvation of the civilian populations through the blockading of ports, and the picture is complete. We had redefined hell.

After three years of this insanity, the two sides had exhausted each other financially, physically, emotionally, and spiritually. At this time, the Americans came into the fray with fresh eager troops and tipped the balance in the Allies' favor. The German economy collapsed and "the-war-to-end-all-wars" was over.

This was the perfect time for our objective powers to come to the forefront. We could organize under the League of Nations and outlaw war forever. Woodrow Wilson, the American president, tried to get the major powers to set aside their emotional need for revenge and be adult about the whole thing.

England and France were not about to let a "Johnny-come-lately" run the show. The war had bankrupted England and France emotionally as well as financially. They subjectively needed to blame and punish. It is the way we are programmed. When we make a mistake we must blame someone else — we can't take the status loss. Denial steps in and we point a finger at another.

The same sort of thing happened in America. America had lucked out. The war had not been fought on American land. America was not in the war long enough to make it a heavy financial burden. America came away as a status winner, with much excitement and comparatively few casualties. America was not about to stick around and clean up the mess. In spite of the LEAGUE OF NATIONS being the American president's personal cause for future world peace, the American people voted against even joining the League of Nations. America was in denial.

At the peace conference at the end of the war, severe reparations were imposed on a devastated German people — our programmed need to exact revenge. Germany could hardly feed its people, let alone pay vast sums to the Allies. In spite of all the economic burdens, the German government started to recover, only to fall into heavy inflation, social unrest, and finally financial collapse.

Off the streets of Vienna steps Adolph Hitler — a sociopathic discontent with criminal tendencies. Under normal circumstances, he would have been hooted off the stage. But to a humiliated, broken, postwar Germany, he offered pugnacious redemption. Hitler promised rejection of the Allied reparations, a new army, and the blaming of Germany's defeat on the Jewish population. He would restore respect, status, and pride once again to the German people.

The German people would follow anyone who could to get their respect back. Hitler instinctively knew this. He promised to defy the allied peace agreement and re-arm, giving back to the German people the world status they had enjoyed before the war. Upon taking power, Hitler used brutality, propaganda, and control of the press to take over the government. He got everyone working on massive government building projects and stabilized the economy. At first he hid the re-arming of Germany, then burst into the open with defiance of the peace agreements that had been imposed on the humbled German people.

In a few masterful strokes, Hitler used our ancient programming to give pride back to the German people — and they made him a God. This is pure human programming. We are programmed to follow a decisive strong leader. With respect and status, a nation has life, motivation, and energy. Without status, a nation has only humiliation and depression. The people of Germany were so grateful to get their status and pride back that they enthusiastically gave Hitler total control.

Hitler is a textbook case of the possible uses of our human animal programming for generating group energy and cohesion. He used our programmed need for racial purity, supernatural heroes, pageantry, rituals, and violence to capture the people's sense of ancient STATUS. Hitler painted Germany as a victim of international bullying that he would punish the world for — US AND THEM. He then used the Jews as the scapegoat for the loss of the First World War — DENIAL. Hitler had tripped all the human programming triggers, giving Germany unity, motivation, and energy while the other nations of the world were questioning their politics and social responsibilities.

With the advent of the industrial revolution and unregulated capitalism, horrible working conditions for the factory workers had existed throughout the nineteenth century and into the twentieth. There was child labor, starvation wages, and terrible living conditions in all the industrial nations.

Remember, we are programmed to live in egalitarian societies. The rising middle classes were living in comfortable houses with domestic servants, while the working masses were stacked in unhealthy slums. There was a discontent in the working classes that was about to boil over. In the second half of the First World War, the Russian people revolted, killed off their royal family, and set up a communist Russian government. All the European countries were facing labor unrest, discontent with Royalty and capitalism, and the threat of communism.

To the intelligentsia, as well as the working masses of the world, capitalism seemed to have failed. Under capitalism there were boom and bust cycles that caused mass unemployment and periodic starvation. There were big money trade wars brought on by capitalist greed. The communist philosophy — *"From each according to his ability to each according to their need"* — made sense logically. If we made a classless society and all pulled together, everyone could live a decent life. It seemed self-evident, but our programming was not taken into account. We can't live in a classless society. Status is how we are organized and motivated. It is the main goal in our lives. We can't change that. We must accommodate our programmed need for status.

The people of Europe were considering communism. If capitalism could lead them into the hell of the First World War, maybe it was time to try a new type of government. This movement scared the European upper classes and the industrialists. What could they do? Hitler would show them. He outlawed unions, assassinated the Communist leaders, beat their followers in the streets, and imposed strict law and order.

There was no denying it. Hitler had taken a defeated Germany in emotional, social, financial, and spiritual ruin and turned it into a proud vibrant nation, while defeating the communist threat at the same time. The other governments of Europe were having union troubles and communist unrest. They were so impressed with what Hitler had accomplished that they couldn't help but admire him.

America at this time was trying to climb out of the depression of the thirties. There were union battles, massive unemployment, and bread lines. Franklin Delano Roosevelt had been elected president. America has been lucky. In times of social confusion and danger a great leader has come forth and steadied the ship of state — Washington, Lincoln, and now Roosevelt.

FDR could see that capitalism was the best form of government. It fit our programming. It rewarded ambition, gave people status goals and challenges with rewards — "life, liberty, and the pursuit of happiness." The big problem with capitalism was that if it wasn't controlled, it was prone to boom and bust with the rich getting richer and the poor getting poorer. FDR knew that a strong central government could be the control that capitalism needed.

Against the powerful interests of industry, finance, and tradition, FDR moved America toward a more egalitarian society. He instituted vast public works programs getting people back to work and money back in circulation. He got congress to pass laws to control big business, the stock market, and to provide for the people's social security. It was rough sledding. It was the war in Europe that really got America going again.

Hitler is the story of the Second World War. He single-handedly got the whole world bashing each other's brains out. The other western nations were afraid of war, having not fully recovered from the last one. Even Hitler's generals were against a new war, but it was too late.

Hitler successfully used the intimidation of his new army to get back German lands and people by promising to stop as soon as he had reunited Germany. He made a non-aggression pact with the Russians to secure his back. He then trumped up a shooting war with Poland, thinking the English and French would not have the guts to declare war even though they were obliged to come to Poland's aid by international treaty. England and France had no choice. The Allies did declare war. The Second World War was on.

Hitler's war machine initially had great success sweeping through Western Europe in months, leaving only England to fight on. Hitler was stopped by the English Channel and the Royal Air Force. Hitler knew intuitively that time was temporarily on his side. He needed to keep going while the other nations were still rearming. He turned on Russia even though he had a non-aggression pact with them (this is animal programming — if we have one success we emotionally believe we will have more successes). Hitler, high on his easy victories in the west, ended up believing his own invincibility propaganda. He plunged into Russia, sure he could defeat them in a couple of months.

About this same time the Japanese, who had been at war with China since the thirties, attacked the United States and took over most of Southeast Asia. The United States declared war on Japan and Germany. The war was now truly worldwide. It took about a year for the United States to get going, but when it did, it was amazing. American mass production supplied two war fronts — the Russians, the English, and the American troops in Europe, and the American and Commonwealth nations in the Pacific.

Hitler had bitten off more than he could chew. Russia was large and stubborn. For most of the Second World War, the Russians were fighting the Germans alone. American history doesn't give Russia the credit it deserves. Even when the "D-DAY" landings were taking place in France, Russia was fighting about two hundred and fifty German divisions. The Germans had only sixty divisions fighting the Americans and the English in the west. It would be fair to say that the Russians, at a staggering human cost, brought the Hitler war machine to its knees.

When the war finally ended, Japan, Russia, and Europe lay in ruin and fifty million people were dead. The shock of the German extermination of the European Jews had taken US AND THEM to moral depths no one could initially believe. The Russians had lost twenty million people and now claimed control over Eastern Europe.

Where the League of Nations had failed after the First World War, the new United Nations was determined to succeed. Unfortunately, the nations of the world only gave lip service to the United Nations, but it was a start. The ink wasn't dry on the peace agreements when new battle lines were being drawn — the Red menace vs. the good guys (more US AND THEM).

America had not only been the "arsenal of democracy," but it had dramatically ended the war by launching the world into the "Atomic Age." This was a product of basic human programming. War is our number one motivator — life or death. The Second World War was the largest concentration of human energy the world had ever experienced. Everyone dropped their petty complaints, pulled together, and worked longer and harder than they had ever done before. It has been estimated that mankind was so motivated by a good vs. evil war, that it produced over a hundred years of technological advances in less than a decade — jet aircraft, plastics, electronics, medicine, exotic metals, rocketry, the computer, atomic energy, and too many other advances to list.

America was on top of the world. It owned this colossal industrial engine that had out-produced the rest of the world. America was flush with victory, unscratched by the war and suddenly the leader of the free world. Having seen what blaming and punishing had done at the end of the First World War, America was smart enough (or scared of the Russians enough) to help rebuild the Axis Powers instead of letting our programmed sense of REVENGE play out. The

Marshal Plan rebuilt and saved the free world. Without the Marshal Plan, western Europe would probably have become communist and set the international community back at least a century.

Communism is a great idea for a logically-run society. It works wonders for the ants. It cannot work for humans. Human programming and organization of our societies is based on STATUS. We must be able to compete for status or we have no motivation, no creativity, and no energy — only confusion and depression. The communist basis is a classless society. It can't work with humans. It never has. Any society that has tried communism has had to resort to a brutal dictatorship to keep the illusion of success going.

It wasn't long before the Russians got the bomb. America's victory party was short-lived. America was no longer the undisputed international top dog. US AND THEM was back in bloom. Paranoia, fear, and patriotism gripped the world. China had gone communist and the rest of Asia looked to be next. The "Red menace" had to be stopped, hence the Korean War.

The Korean War was an emotional disaster. It was christened a "police action" by the United Nations. Everyone was sick of war, but the Red menace had to be stopped. It was a depressing mess, without clearly defined objectives or the chance of a clear-cut victory. As soon as the United Nation's forces started getting the upper hand, the Red Chinese sent masses of troops into the fray on the North Korean side, causing a stalemate that exists to this day. The Russians were allied with the Chinese. It became a standoff. No one was willing to risk the Third World War. We entered into the "cold war," trying to outdo each other with atomic saber-rattling.

It was pure human animal programming. In nature, size matters. All a large animal needs to do is confront a smaller animal and the smaller animal usually backs down. If the two animals are of similar size, a lot of circling, posturing, ground pawing, and threats are exchanged. Energy is high as violence can break out at any instant. It is this atmosphere that has caused the fantastic technological advances we have accomplished in the last fifty years. The space race, the computer sciences, advanced materials, etc., are the result of US AND THEM energy. We are at our most productive when we are motivated by the possibility of war.

The Vietnam War was another unnecessary mess that America never should have gotten into. It was a by-product of paranoia. The US policy makers were afraid that the Red Chinese and the Red Vietnamese would get together and take over the Far East. It was felt that they had to be stopped somewhere. That somewhere was Vietnam.

After eighty thousand American and over one million Vietnamese lay dead, nothing had been accomplished. The political leaders got together to talk over the war about twenty years after the fact. The Vietnamese leader said that there never was a chance that Vietnam would join with the Red Chinese. He explained that they had hated and periodically been at war with each other for two thousand years. The American state department simply hadn't done its homework — yet another classic example of our animal emotional programming overriding logic, research, and analytical deduction.

The scary part of this period of human history is that the United States and the Soviet Union were playing chicken with thousands of hydrogen ICBMS, all pre-targeted for major industrial and population centers. Had all-out war erupted, the mess may never have been cleaned up. Even when destruction of our life support system (our biosphere) is the probable outcome of indulging our emotional US AND THEM, we still don't stop, think it through, and come up with a solution. If we don't get control of our emotional programming, we will self-destruct. Under the auspices of

120

our emotions, we will fight to the death rather than accept a major loss of STATUS. We know better. We just can't help ourselves.

Money is stored human energy. In the last quarter of the twentieth century, the western First World populations were engaged in an exciting, motivating, individual status competition — the "me generation." Add to this the new communication revolution, international jet cargo planes, computers, and the efficient business model, and you have a new level of prosperity. Everything was novel, liberating, and exciting. The birth-control pill removed the taboos on sex. The music was uninhibited. Everyone was motivated, excited, and working hard to buy the necessary status symbols to bolster their pride. It was a celebration of our hedonistic programming — status and sex. The western nations were rich from all the energy.

The Soviet Union at this time was in a state of failed five-year programs and economic and spiritual depression. With television, radio, movies, and magazines showing the ongoing western party, the Soviet citizens were no longer motivated by nationalistic US AND THEM. They wanted to join the party. It wasn't military might that brought down the Berlin Wall — it was Levi's, rock music, and consumer goods.

With the collapse of the Red menace, political philosophers were worried. Without an outside threat — without US AND THEM — could America maintain its motivation and pride? Not to worry. The Middle East would fill the void.

As far as religions go, Islam is hard to argue with. They don't allow advertising, sleeping with other men's wives, lending money on interest, or scantily dressed women in public. The western world was not only running their party on Middle Eastern oil, but the party itself was a direct violation of everything Islam held sacred.

To top off this international rebuff of Islamic values was the situation with Israel. At the end of the Second World War, the western powers gave the Jewish people a homeland in the center of the Islamic world. Israel immediately became a First World nation. The Jewish refugees from Europe were well educated, and highly motivated.

The Arabs had controlled this land for over a thousand years. Now the Jewish people were transforming the desert into fruit orchards and farms. Modern cities were emerging and the Arabs were being upstaged. The Arabs were having status and self-confidence problems before the Jews arrived. Now they had no status at all. This is straight programming. A people cannot function without status or pride. The Arabs had to get their self-worth back. They would wipe the intruders out.

The Arab nations outnumbered the Israelis forty-to-one, but it was still a one-sided affair. The Arabs were Second and Third World nations fighting a First World nation. They attacked but were beaten again and again. They were humiliated again and again and just got madder and madder. The hate that the Arab world has for the First World nations in general, and the Jewish people in particular, is so vast that it can't be measured. Since the Jewish state owes much of its existence to the American-Jewish community, the Arabs can't help but have a special hatred for America.

This gets right down into the dark parts of our human emotional programming. When people are denied their dignity, pride, and self-confidence, something deep inside snaps. The BBC aired a documentary on a Palestinian training school for child suicide bombers — madness. They also conducted an interview with the family of a suicide bomber who had died in an attack on Israel. When asked what their feelings were about the loss of their father and husband, the family replied that they were disappointed that he had only killed two Israelis.

This is truly blind hate — they are practicing death because of dishonor. Reason is nowhere in the equation. The Arabs and Persians are not inferior madmen. It is instructive to see that anyone would more than likely behave in a similar manner if they were internationally humiliated, marginalized, and discounted.

All this Middle Eastern madness was paralleled by the rise of the American religious far right. Clever Republican operatives saw a chance to take over American politics with the help of middle-American insecurity. Change was happening too fast.

People wanted to go back to the old America — the America with strong families, religious values, and a predominantly white population. They yearned for the time when being a God-fearing family man was the national model of success and stability. Of course that is impossible. No one can ever really go back. Life is an ever-changing organism. The only constant in life is change.

The American paranoia swept into office a self-proclaimed "born again Christian" — George W. Bush. This man, through his unshakable religious faith, was going to lead America back to the nineteen fifties and put out the Middle Eastern fires. George W. Bush is an intelligent, energetic, and positive man. If I were to meet him, I am sure we would get along. But it has been said that even a genius in the wrong job can be less than adequate.

George Bush isn't a bad person, he is just in the wrong job. He would make a great general manager of a NFL football team. His energy and faith would be an inspiration to the team and I am sure he would do well. A football team is one hundred percent subjective animal programming — a symbolic life and death band war.

The Middle East is a complicated cultural, psychological, religious, and emotional mess that has been brewing for centuries. There is no possible military victory.

Military intervention has only deepened the void and solidified the hate and social rage.

What the Middle East people want is to get their pride back. They were one of the most respected and admired regions in the world eight hundred years ago. They have money and resources through their oil, but very little to none of it trickles down to the man on the street. Money alone cannot buy status and respect. Remember, human beings must have at least a little status and respect or they will be shunned and socially cease to exist.

Whether it is Iraq, Iran, Afghanistan, or Palestine, the Bush administration's policy has been one of military victory and then forced democracy. First kick their butts, then cram democracy down their throats. A simple and, they believe, effective plan. We will save them whether they like it or not.

By definition, this policy could never work. Our programming doesn't allow us to be happily dominated by others. Humans are also programmed to revere their ancestors. We have an emotional attachment to the history of our band and a strong genetic inclination to do what we have always done. People cannot change overnight. In fact we can't change in a generation. We are programmed to maintain the status quo.

The answers to this situation are not cosmic secrets, but academic common knowledge. The social sciences have come a long way in the last couple of decades. Blind faith, unexamined emotions, and denial have gotten the world into this mess. More of the same cannot get us out.

Here we are near the end of the first decade of a new millennium. The Middle East is a caldron of hate, confusion, and desperation. There are still thousands of hydrogen bombs in ICBMs targeting the major cities of the world. The pollution of the first world nations is having a measurable effect on the strength and patterns of the weather. We are poisoning our water supplies with heavy metals. We are strip-fishing the oceans. We have overpopulated the earth with people. We are decimating wild animal populations and their habitats. We are hard at work destroying our life support system and picking up momentum every day. We are programmed emotional animals and can't seem to stop ourselves. I believe we can. I believe we can break our denial, use our logic, knowledge, imagination, and the neuroplasticity of our brains to save ourselves from ourselves.

PART THREE

HOW CAN WE SAVE OUR PLANET AND OURSELVES?

WE MUST BREAK THROUGH our faith and denial that is keeping our animal programming in control. As soon as we get beyond our programmed human centric view of the world, we can see that a balanced nature is the only way forward. We have to let go of our stranglehold on the biosphere and let it breath again.

First, we must start the foundations of a meaningful World Government. The United Nations would seem to be the best candidate, as it is already up and running. We must give the UN teeth and international respect. Second, through a new United Nations, we must address three main areas: POPULATION, POLLUTION, and TERRORISM.

I believe the first step is to take the existing United Nations, strip it down to its sub floor, and rebuild it. Over the next two or three decades, we need to establish the UN as the future seat of world government. The time to start the conversion, from a patchwork of feuding nations to world government is now. The UN must be dedicated to the welfare of all human beings. It must have an equitable international world court justice system. It must have the only large military force in the world. The UN must be the biosphere's watchdog and protector — good luck!

This sounds like delusional madness, much like getting a group of cats to march in a parade. Here again, much time is needed to get people to even think in this way. We need great leaders and ongoing public relations campaigns to see through our denial and get started. The time is now. The time is short.

The big problem is that we must do what our programming dictates. We are programmed to fight wars with neighboring bands. We are programmed to use violence in extreme emotional situations. We are programmed to fight nature for our existence.

It would seem that what is needed now is a long-term elaborate social experiment to prove the hypothesis that humanity can adapt from our programmed emotional need for war with our neighbors to abiding by a system of equitable laws. We need to prove that we can change from "BRING IT ON" to a legal position of "SEE YOU IN COURT." Not to worry, the work has already been done. We have a two-hundred-year study and ongoing experiment that, to my mind, proves the point — THE UNITED STATES OF AMERICA.

The United States of America is not perfect. But then no system of government can be perfect. Human life is a living thing. It cannot be pinned down to one immutable set of rules and work forever. That is where the United States and the other First World democracies shine. They have a living set of laws. They are being updated and improved on a daily basis through elected representatives of the people.

Where the United States, in its beginnings, had an advantage over its European predecessors is that it started off its life with no old baggage holding it back. America didn't have to fight established royal families and rigid class systems. There is a class system of a sort, but an open, mobile class system. Anyone from any background can climb the American status ladder. America also has a vast raw country of many natural resources.

It is almost a perfect social experiment; put a few million chance-taking people with a desire to rule themselves in a large country of untapped resources; mix thoroughly, let it brew for two hundred years, and see what happens. What happened was a bumpy ride. There was political corruption, financial robber barons, slavery, a civil war, segregation, union strife, woman's rights, and on and on. Through it all, over time, the people prevailed — hammering out, law after law, a good way of life through its elected officials. The building of a sound democracy is a long and complicated process. Much fighting, compromising, and just the passage of time is needed.

The time has come for a meaningful world government. I believe the First World democracies can be used as a working example of what could be done with world government. If there were only First World nations, there would be no war or terrorism today. No, this cannot be accomplished in the next decade, but the time to start laying the foundations is here.

The whole world is much smaller today than the United States was only sixty years ago. Sixty years ago it took over a week to get from America to Europe if you made perfect travel connections. Travel to the Orient was measured in months. It was possible to call overseas on the telephone, but the process was time-consuming, problematic, and prohibitively expensive. The world is no longer a world of distant strange lands. Television, the Web, movies, and instant communication has the world, more or less, reaching for the same life — a democratic government responsive to its people.

In the United States there are fifty states, many as large as a European country, living peaceably side-by-side. There is no possibility of California going to war with Oregon. Constantly updated laws and an equitable justice system have taken the place of violence in the settling of disputes. The United States has been accused of overdoing law (America has about seven times as many lawyers as the average country). Remember, without law and order, civilization is not possible. If an American feels another has wronged him, there is legal recourse. A citizen can even sue the government. Americans don't riot and bring the government down every time they disagree with policy. If they feel disenfranchised, they rally the vote and change the laws.

Our programmed call to war has been taken out of America's interstate disagreements and channeled into sports — football, basketball, baseball, hockey, soccer, et al. On the weekend, millions attend sporting events of their choosing and experience all the confrontational emotional rush of US AND THEM.

Tens of millions follow the fortunes of their sports heroes on television, often with friends and beer. We form strong bonds with our teams, going on emotional roller coaster rides with the ebb and flow of the physical battle. That is the saving grace of our programmed violent emotions. We can transfer our programmed need to war with our neighboring bands onto the sports fields, while retaining all the competitive emotional excitement of a life and death confrontation. At the conclusion of the weekend, no one is dead. Our emotions have been excited to a fevered pitch and nothing has been destroyed.

The United States also has a provision for our objective side — our wizard mind. The American system of laws assures as much intellectual freedom as possible. One can do or say almost anything as long as it doesn't injure another. Everyone is given a basic education and is encouraged to seek higher education. More money is spent on research and development in the United States than in any other country. Small business and innovation are encouraged. If a person is academically gifted, they can apply for research grants and scholarships. Copyrights and patents assure the individual ownership of their artistic and intellectual creations. This all fits in with our programming. We are programmed to seek individual status within our band. We must express our individuality while supporting our family and band.

The United States has been able to get fifty small countries (states) to work together under one political, monetary, and legal system. All these states have many religious denominations and ethnic groups from every corner of the world. Not only can all these people peaceably share this diversity, but also have a good chance to achieve personal happiness while doing it. Americans are among the happiest populations in the world.

We need to get social scientists, politicians, and philosophers from all over the world to redesign the United Nations. We have proven that it can be done. Again, there is no threat of war right now among the First World countries. If there were only First World countries there would be no war. Like the states within the United States, the countries of the First World, while having trade disputes and ideological differences, do not even contemplate the possibility of war against each other.

Once the new United Nations is set on a course of becoming the seat of World Government, a program to encourage and facilitate the gradual change from theocracies, oligarchies, and warlord governments to democracies must be a top priority. Where governments control information and dictate to mind and body, rabid patriotism and religious bigotry flourish, creating destructive US AND THEM situations that inevitably turn to border wars and armed oppression. Third World governments must be helped to evolve into elected parliamentary types of governments that embrace personal welfare and freedom of information.

The new United Nations must be designed, financed, and empowered to be the seat of world government and the only world military power. The philosophy must be one of working together for a better world. We must embrace the goal of a better life for all populations and a policy for sustaining the health of the biosphere. The time for coddling and halfhearted efforts to transfer power to the people of Second and Third World governments is over. We must get the international community committed to a war on ignorance, poverty, and self-serving dictators. The trillion dollars that was wasted on the Iraq war could have been used to move failing rogue governments out of the dark ages.

Afghanistan is a good example. If the United Nations had put enough troops on the ground to establish law and order, collect all the military arms and build a government infrastructure, Afghanistan could have been saved. This wouldn't have been a quick fix. It takes decades for people to adapt to a new social order. The troops would need to be in-country for years. Great pains would need to be taken to assure that the population would not get the social bends. Long-held social conventions would have to be respected and changed slowly. We are programmed to do things the way we have always done things. It will take a good amount of time for a population that has been under the heel of warlords to understand and participate in a democracy.

To start with, the United Nations would need to run a Third World country with experienced teams of advisors for at least five years. Elections would have to wait until law and order was well established and a competent police force was trained and in place. The UN troops and the government advisors could be reduced gradually. It would take at least a decade to get Afghanistan on its feet and on its own. Once people experience control over their lives and social order, they feel motivated, empowered, and proud — it is all in our programming.

I know this sounds simplistic and of course has been proposed before. The whole world has been giving lip service to outlawing war and establishing world peace for years. It has all been idealistic wishful thinking. The big difference now is that we are toying with the destruction of nature and we have nowhere to move. The human species is up against the wall. We either have to resign ourselves to eventual self-destruction or use an outside perspective to channel the destructive aspects of our Stone Age programming into benign activities. We must become the caretakers of our biosphere

A strong UN is needed to save the biosphere from the human animals. I admit that a strong UN is a Herculean task in itself; some would say impossible. But this is a time of extreme emergency. It will take probably fifty years to save ourselves from ourselves if we start right now. What we are doing right now is the "frog in the pan" experiment. If a frog is placed in a pan of water on an operating burner, the frog will not sense the raising temperature, hop out, and save himself. He will serenely float about and eventually die in boiling water.

We are not paying attention. We are in danger. We are our own enemy. We are in DENIAL. With or without a strong UN, we must aggressively address three main areas of human destructive behavior: POPULATION, POLLUTION, and TERRORISM.

Population

"For millions of years human beings simply went at nature with everything they had, scrounging food and fighting off predators across a known world of a few square miles. Life was short, fate terrifying, and reproduction an urgent priority: children, if freely conceived, just about replaced the family members who seemed to be dying all the time. The population flickered around equilibrium, and sometimes whole bands became extinct. Nature was something out there — nameless and limitless, a force to beat against, cajole, and exploit."

— E.O. Wilson

Population is possibly the biggest hurdle man has to conquer. All of our current world problems are the direct result of human overpopulation. The whole point of animal programming is to get our genes into the next generation. The point of life is more life. Sex and procreation is one of our strongest sets of programmed imperatives. It is at the heart of our great religions — "go forth and be fruitful." Any attempt to control our numbers is met with denial. If the subject of population control is pushed, it is met with rebellion and violence. The subject is so loaded that no politician will touch it with a barge pole.

All animals are programmed to reproduce to about one hundred and ten percent of the available food supplies. This all works out well in the realm of nature's checks and balances. The strongest feed and the weakest die — straight Darwinian evolution. The current problem is that man is no longer living within the realm of nature. We have overpowered nature and have struck out on our own. We are now using nature as source material for our technological worldwide consumer economy — to feed, shelter, and amuse our runaway numbers.

The world — the biosphere — is a large living organism that has fallen prey to a cancer. The cancer is the human race. We have, through our own cleverness, expanded our food supplies while devastating the habitats of other life forms. For our first fifty-thousand years on earth, the number of human animals was about five to ten million worldwide. We are now above six billion. There are a thousand times as many human beings as there were when we lived in nature in our naturally occurring numbers.

The only thing that is wrong with this planet is too many people. Not only are our numbers a huge burden on the balance of the biosphere, but we are engaged in numerous damaging activities — destroying rain forests, burning fossil fuels, mining metals, and producing chemicals in volumes and concentrations that never occur in nature.

Nature has a natural resilience. If damaged, nature can heal itself in a relatively short time. A good example is the volcanic eruption of Mount Saint Helens in the northwestern United States. It was the biggest eruption recorded in modern times. Scientists were amazed at how quickly the damage was repaired by nature. Twenty years later and it is a reconstituted part of the biosphere. The problem we now face is that the damage human activities are wreaking upon the biosphere are ongoing. We never let up. The damage humans are inflicting on nature are festering sores that only get larger every year. The damage never stops. Nature never gets a chance to heal.

We think of the world as being "bigger than all outdoors." No. The world is too small to handle the number of people it has now. According to scientists, the human population should top out at about thirteen billion around the end of this century. This is madness. This will be double the current population.

Our atmosphere is now losing its protective ozone layer. The global warming has already caused the world's weather to become measurably more violent. All this can be traced back to the fact that our biosphere cannot support the human numbers it has now.

There is a farmyard rule of thumb that illustrates this situation. If a farmer puts one cow for every acre of pasture, the cows will be content and the pasture will be lush and green. Put a hundred cows to the acre and the cows will starve in a quagmire of filth.

Viewed from a logical outside perspective, solving human overpopulation is a no-brainer. We have contraceptives. All we have to do is set population parameters that keep the human population in a nondestructive range. If we were logical (instead of emotional), we would require that a couple who desire to have a child fill out an application showing that they could provide food, shelter, and love for the child to be. When an opening in the population appeared, the pregnancy could begin.

The howl of human disapproval can only be imagined. The worlds' religions support, through their ancient texts, unlimited human offspring. Women have a programming that demands that they mate and have children. Men are programmed to mate with as many women as they can. In most cultures a man's status is to some degree dependent on the number of children he has sired. In our prehistoric band days, where we struggled to survive, having as many children as possible was the only way for the band to continue.

Hunter-gatherer bands had a fifty percent infant mortality at birth. Starvation, parasites, and diseases ravaged them; they had forty times as many violent deaths as today and life expectancy was around thirty-five years of age. With an all out effort, it was an iffy thing to keep the band at one hundred and fifty individuals. This state of affairs was the norm for over ninety-nine percent of the time humans have been on earth. Rampant reproduction is in our genetic instructions, in all our ancient cultures and religions, creating belief systems that view unlimited reproduction as a duty.

Today with modern medicine, high-tech agriculture, and a world economy, population has gotten out of control and no one dares mention the fact. This is where an empowered UN could begin an education campaign and open negotiations with religious leaders. This is one of those situations where a good amount of time is needed to turn this situation around. It will take generations to get measurable results. The time to start is now.

Pollution

Pollution is almost exclusively a First World sin. A First World person's way of life burns hundreds of times the amount of fossil fuels (in cars, houses, through his consumer goods, and in the maintenance of his community infra-structure) as a Third World person. Our new First World way of life is power intensive and we get power primarily through the burning of gas, oil, and coal. We are dumping greenhouse gasses into our atmosphere in substantial and ever-increasing amounts. China and India are racing to the First Worlds' levels of per-capita pollution. The East, with the largest block of the world's population and the fewest environmental restrictions, is about to double and redouble pollution in the next couple of decades. If we were to let up for twenty years, our biosphere would have a chance to recover but the forecast is only for massive increases.

The world's scientific community has been tearing its hair out and screaming to the politicians that we are causing massive damage to the biosphere that must be controlled. How many times have we watched politicians on TV say that curbing pollution is too expensive. Too expensive? This would be humorous if it wasn't so destructive and pathetic. For a politician to propose meaningful legislation to curb greenhouse gasses, with its attendant costs, would be to commit political suicide.

To stay in the political arena, a politician must appeal to a population that is in denial. Through our denial we are actively fouling our nest and destroying our habitat, while some political leaders are maintaining that it hasn't been proven that pollution has adversely affected our biosphere.

"We really don't have to address this so-called problem. We can keep our way of life and cheap gasoline too — vote for me."

Our consumer way of life is like an addictive drug. The more we get, the more we want. We now regard our standard of living as a birthright. "To take my consumer way of life from me you will have to pry it from my cold dead hands." We instinctively go into denial when we hear about our damage to the environment. "I don't see any damage." "I didn't do any polluting." We are programmed to display as much status as we can and modern status is mostly about the quantity and quality of the consumer goods we possess. On top of our status demands, we are programmed to think about only the next six months.

Pollution is a problem of conservation and the monitoring of nature for decades and centuries. The problem of pollution confronts some of our basic programmed imperatives — status, being in the now, and our instinctive view of nature as our adversary. Nature is our programmed challenge not our programmed responsibility. When pollution is mentioned, we get hit with a triple dose of denial.

The whole world is turning to the consumer economy as a way of life. This isn't right or wrong, it is an expression of our programming. The consumer economy provides jobs, competition, and self-expression — all programmed human needs.

There is a scientific economic proposal that is gaining favor. The idea is to require all consumer goods to be made of completely recyclable materials. New products would be manufactured with the recycled materials used to build the last round of consumer goods. At one stroke we would reduce mining, pollution, and trash. New industries and jobs would be created and we could go on with our "show and tell" status lives while greatly reducing our impact on the biosphere. Under the present political climate this proposal is impossible. The public and industry would never stand for this fundamental shift. We are programmed to do things the way we have always done them. America has the most successful government in the world. It is responsive to and supportive of our human emotional needs, but it is poor at responding to our biosphere's objective needs.

I propose that the time has come for the United States to create a new branch of our government. Along with the executive, judicial, and legislative we need to add the scientific. Science is the only human endeavor that is nòt dominated by our programmed emotions.

Even with THE SCIENTIFIC METHOD, we have to watch ourselves carefully. Science is full of stories of the fudging of findings and results to fit the intended conclusions. America's recent history is a case of politicians ignoring all the scientific advice they are given. Politicians view science as a rival power base trying to horn in on their decision-making process.

The whole Middle East conflict is a case for social scientists to play a substantial role. But no. It is much like getting the branches of the military to cooperate. They will not do it. There are power bases to protect and turf to defend (status and US AND THEM). They are human. Their programming demands that they keep the ground they have and fight for more.

With the new branch of SCIENCE added to the structure of the American government, logic would finally have a fighting chance. There are many things that should not be left up to the emotionally-driven general public to decide at the polls. The new branch would be able to strike down any legislation that would bring damage to the biosphere and have the power to introduce needed legislation to maintain the biosphere. At last, important decisions could be made based on facts and logical deduction rather then on emotions.

I can imagine the new SCIENCE branch of the American government as being much like the judicial. There could be a court of perhaps seven scientists appointed by the president to serve life terms. The nominees would have to be prominent working scientists and subject to confirmation by the senate.

With this new branch of government, many pollution problems could at last be addressed. For example, one of the biggest pollution problems — gasoline consumption — could be cut in half in less than a decade. The American representative government has been in complete denial about the price of gasoline for over half a century. In Europe, through taxes, gasoline has been over five dollars a gallon for decades. Unlimited cheap gasoline is considered an American birth right. Add to this the fact that worldwide, personal automobiles are status statements more than they are transportation. We have a world full of overpowered monster cars and trucks. In nature, status goes to the large and powerful — size matters.

American political leaders have been told of the gradual destruction of the biosphere through greenhouse gasses for over fifty years. The emotionally-driven public must display their status. The number one status symbol is a prestige automobile. Bigger is always more and more is status and power. What people fail to see is that status is a relative thing. If everyone were forced by legislation to fifty-mile-to-the-gallon transportation there would still be prestige cars — marvels of technology, style, and desirability. We could still strut our stuff and burn less than half the fossil fuels we burn today.

The key to getting people to do what is best for the environment is to appeal to their status — find a way to financially reward them. People will enthusiastically do anything for money. Example: the nationwide roadsides used to be littered with beer and pop bottles and cans. By legislating a small deposit on each bottle and can, redeemable at recycling centers, the whole problem was solved. So it would be if there were substantial financial incentives to buy a fuel-efficient car.

If America had a scientific branch of government, America could have a national gas tax that would go up twenty-five cents a gallon every year until it reached three or four dollars a gallon. This would make gas prices in the six to seven dollar a gallon range. The outrage would be substantial. But people will not save or respect anything unless they pay dearly for it.

Everyone would have a decade to buy a more fuel-efficient car. The scientific community would have an immediate challenge to build the most efficient and clean burning cars possible (the major car companies can produce comfortable quick cars that get over fifty miles to the gallon right now). Since cars and trucks currently average less than twenty miles to the gallon, gasoline consumption would be more than cut in half and actually cost the consumer less of a percentage of their budget than it does today. The resulting high cost of automobile fuels would encourage people to ride bikes, walk on short distance trips, and use mass transit. People would get more exercise, spend more time in their community, and as a result, less fuel would be consumed. A three or four dollar a gallon gas tax would raise a huge amount of money (in the trillions of dollars) that could be shared by federal governments and the new United Nations. This large amount of money could be used to finance education, population and pollution control, and wildlife conservation worldwide.

Terrorism

The disenfranchised let terrorists loose on the First World because they have reached the point of ego rage. If they can't get respect they will throw a destructive fit.

Negative attention is better than no attention at all. They don't have enough ethnic pride — a respected place in the international community. They are mad as hell and they are not going to take it any longer. They are so frustrated that they have become self-destructive.

The world is now so small that no country can exist in isolation. Example: Julia Roberts was on a trip to the deep African outback. She came to an ancient mud hut village with no services or electricity. She got out of her SUV. A loincloth-clad native approached and said, "pretty woman."

This is all about basic human programming. The foundation of ethnic religious mental stability is a shared belief system that gives the individual and his band a sense of status. People used to live happy lives without electricity, shopping, and consumer goods. Only fifty years ago, societies could live in isolation but that is no longer a possibility. The First World culture is being broadcast by satellite over the whole world. Television, DVDs, IPods, cell phones, and assorted electronic gadgets have made isolation impossible. First World culture is here to stay and growing stronger every day.

Human programming doesn't allow for a different but equal social status. Status goes with the power. There is only one status way of life and that is First World. You either must join the First World or die trying to fight it. Unfortunately the Middle East is dying trying to fight for its self-respect. They are in a classic double bind. They hate the First World living style yet realize that it is the world standard of international status. They instinctively want status yet hate the way it is being expressed.

A psychology experiment was conducted using two groups of preschool children. The two groups were placed in adjacent rooms with a glass wall and curtain separating them. One group was given a broken chair, wood scraps, some old spoons, pans, and a large sandbox. The second group was given all the new remote-controlled cars, Barbie dolls, and upscale toys. The children started playing with the toys at hand. After each group of children was happily at play, the curtain was pulled back so that the two groups could see each other but not interact. The group of children with the broken chair, wood scraps, and sandbox had been having a wonderful time until they saw the expensive high-tech toys of the other group. They stopped their play, watched the high-tech group, and turned on the chair, pans, and wood scraps with angry violence, then sat in despair.

This experiment is a microcosm of our present international discord. The Arab and Persian countries are analogous to the children with the wood scraps and the sandbox. As soon as they see that there is a more prestigious way to play, they feel a complete loss of status. This leads to frustration, violence, and depression. This is our programming. We can't be happy without a sense of status for ourselves and our band.

The Islamic fundamentalists want to turn the clock back to the first millennium, where they were in the high-tech group with power and international status. Proud dynamic men who were respected in the world ran their religion and their culture. Now they are called towel heads and wogs. They know through TV and movies that they are out of the power game. They are a century behind in infrastructure and national economies. Human programming demands that they compete, but they are in a status battle they cannot win. They are striking out blindly. They don't even have an agenda. They just want to destroy the infidels that are undermining their status and marginalizing their religious way of life.

On to the world stage steps George W. Bush. He, with his Texas Wild West manhood and his recently acquired fundamental Christian faith, will solve this cultural impasse with manly bold strokes. First he divides the conflict into

US AND THEM — the Godly good guys and the axis of evil. He then cuts off all dialogue — these people are not worth talking to. Then he teaches them a military lesson — don't mess with a Texan. When the UN and the rest of the First World became alarmed, he ran roughshod over them. Stand aside and let a real man handle this.

Right down the line, George W. Bush played out our Stone Age US AND THEM programming — calling nations derogatory names, refusing to even talk to them and then giving them a lopsided military thumping. This is not the best possible plan. What the Arab and Persian worlds are seeking is acceptance and respect. Every one of George Bush's moves has been to humiliate, isolate, and shame. George Bush is not a bad person. George Bush is a born-again Christian in complete denial. He only listens to his animal instincts and Christian dogma.

We are all the same people. Again, there is only one-thousandth of a percentage point difference between the DNA of all humans. There is more genetic variation in a typical baboon troop then there is in the whole human race. The only difference between any people is their social-ization — their belief system.

If you or I were born and raised in a Middle Eastern Islamic nation, we would be furious with the First World nations for stripping us of our international self-respect. In order to bring the Middle Eastern conflict to a positive conclusion, it is imperative that we talk to and listen to the Islamic countries. We must assure them that we are not trying to take their religion or their status away from them.

We do not want to dictate their way of life. We want to empower them and include them in the world family of nations. We must give them time, help, and encouragement through the United Nations. All they want is RESPECT. We must put the big military moves away. Beating them up and further humiliation only enrages them more. Every time we knock them down, they only get up madder. We need to spend the same money on humanitarian aid and assistance to a gradual shift to a more egalitarian form of government.

The Muppets TV shows are a great example of what can be done. The Muppets shows are broadcast all over the Middle East in their native language and are very popular. They show that the United States is a giving and understanding country — even lovable. They put a personal one-on-one face on America. More of the Muppet style of entertainment and communication along with the distribution of humanitarian aide should be employed. The First World needs to work with the Islamic nations in their language and culture rather than dictate and bully. It is the people we need to win over, not the corrupt governments. To listen, understand, respect, and include the Middle Eastern people and their religions in the world of nations is the only way to stop terrorism.

WHY ARE WE
SELF-DESTRUCTING?

OUR WIZARD BRAIN has come late to us. Our mind is a two-part system and the two parts don't really work together yet. Our animal emotions are millions of years old and our large cerebral cortex is only about one hundred thousand years old. Our big brain is new on the scene and hasn't had time to establish itself on an equal footing with our emotions. Our animal emotion side still has its hands on our controls and our wonderful brain is sort of along for the ride. This unfortunate set of circumstances is causing us to inadvertently damage our biosphere while emotionally denying any part in the process.

All animals are programmed to exploit their niche in nature. They are also programmed to reproduce to one hundred and ten percent of the available food supply. That is exactly what we are doing. In our animal lives on the savanna, life was so hazardous that we had to concentrate on reproduction just to raise enough children to keep our band numbers at one hundred fifty. Today, the biosphere is plagued by human overpopulation.

With the use of our large brain we have created technology. Technology has given us the power to break out of nature's framework and appropriate the entire biosphere for our own uses. With our scientific powers, we have reconfigured the world to predominantly support unlimited human reproduction. Unfortunately, we are not giving enough consideration to the health of the biosphere. The biosphere is a living organism and is, like any living thing, susceptible to illness and even death.

The parents of a teenage boy discovered that their child had become addicted to hard drugs. They found the most successful doctor in the field of drug rehabilitation and set up an appointment. The doctor took the boy aside and talked with him. When they got back together with the parents the doctor said, "Bring him back in six months. There is nothing I can do for him now. He is still having fun." And so it is with the human race. We can't get through to ourselves yet. We are still having fun.

We don't have time to wait until we are not having fun anymore. Our biosphere needs help now. We have to break through our denial and get to work now. The sciences tell us that we may be on the threshold of doing damage that neither we nor nature may be able to fix later on. If we continue to focus on our status games without taking serious stock of the ecological damage we are inflicting on the biosphere, we are soon to be in for a rough ride.

Denial keeps us from seeing our own folly. This is straight programming. This is the basis of the Darwinian theory. All animals in nature are programmed to follow their successes until they fail. Then they either adapt to the new situation or go extinct. Science believes that life will, in all likelihood, continue on this planet for billions of years. If we keep disrupting nature's balance, we may not be one of those life forms. Example: the hole in the ozone layer. It was big news a couple of decades ago, but then it started to heal itself after we outlawed fluorocarbons. Now it is growing again and we don't know why. If we lose the ozone layer, the only life on earth will be oceanic or subterranean. Ultraviolet light kills all the living things it shines on.

Humanity is in much the same position as a runaway alcoholic. The meetings of Alcoholics Anonymous start off with, "My name is - - - - - and I am an alcoholic." Until a person can admit to himself and the world that he has a problem, he will keep drinking until he destroys himself. And so it is with humanity. We have to admit to ourselves that we have a problem with our animal programming that is producing overpopulation and pollution. We must see and admit that we are on a path to self-destruction. We have to break through our denial and admit to ourselves, right down to the marrow of our bones, that we have an environmental problem and we are that problem.

Humans, like all animals, are programmed to keep doing whatever works until it fails to work. We are programmed to push it until it breaks. What we are pushing until it breaks is our biosphere. We cannot afford to break our biosphere. We must employ our wizard brain. We must use our logic, science, and foresight to keep this planet's biosphere friendly to its current forms of life. We have to override our faith and denial, see clearly what we are doing, and plan decades and centuries ahead to secure nature's health and our future.

We are, at the moment, in the embarrassing position of having fouled our own nest and having up-ended nature's balance. What is needed is an ongoing, worldwide education and public relations program to get the world's populations on a sustainable path to the future for ourselves and our biosphere.

The key to human motivation is STATUS. We need to mobilize the worlds' celebrities (movie stars, sports heroes, and musicians) to popularize zero emission fuels and alternative transportation options. We must concentrate our efforts on recycling, nature conservancy, and birth control. With the combination of legislated financial incentives and celebrity leadership we could make living green everyone's new status goal.

Part of our human programming is the love of a good challenge — let's use it. If we put one half the energy we put into the cold war, we could have a healthy biosphere by the end of this century. All we need is to empower science to create a plan to save our biosphere and we can start turning our self-destructive programmed tendencies into a secure future for mankind.

> "Can we rely on it that a 'turning around will be accomplished by enough people quickly enough to save the modern world?' This question is often asked, but whatever answer is given to it will mislead. The answer 'yes' would lead to complacency; the answer 'no' to despair. It is desirable to leave these perplexities behind us and get down to work."
> — E.F. Schumacher

EPILOGUE

COLIN POWEL USED THE "Pottery Barn" analogy (if you break it — you own it) to explain to George W. Bush that beating up Iraq was the easy part. I believe this analogy applies to our current relationship with the biosphere. The biosphere is an incredibly complex, intricately interconnected, self-healing organism that was doing fine for four billion years. Then we came along and knocked it off its shelf — interrupting its ecosystems, its balance, and its natural rhythms. We have, if not broken, at least heavily damaged the biosphere and under the Pottery Barn analogy, we now own it. It is now our responsibility. Let us accept this responsibility. Let us step up and do our part so that the biosphere can get on with its own healing. Let us give the biosphere the respect and care it so richly deserves. It is our mother.

We must get our priorities straight. First we must make sure that our great-grandchildren have a hospitable place to live. We don't even have to completely disrupt our current lives. All we need to do is make a few adjustments to our behaviors. We can, with a little effort, assure a positive future for this beautiful biosphere and the human race.

We are in a timed race. We are losing. We could be on the edge of doing environmental damage that we may not be able to fix later. We could be approaching an environmental tipping point. Once we push our biosphere over that edge, we may be helpless to save it. Our biosphere may become something else and we don't know if the new biosphere will support our way of life.

This is particularly ironic in that the human race is on the brink of a golden age. We are just beginning an age of fantastic technological breakthroughs and more people are participating in culture, art, and education than ever before. We are about to blossom at the same time we are destroying our life support system.

With only three comparatively small modifications to our current lifestyle, we can give our over-taxed biosphere a chance to heal itself. We don't even have to fix it. Nature is self-healing if we would only give it a breather.

FIRST: POPULATION. The most important challenge, and the hardest for us to accept, is overpopulation. We must get the United Nations involved in a worldwide educational program to introduce contraceptives and get the world's religions to take unlimited human reproduction out of their canon. All the biosphere's problems are directly connected to human overpopulation. There is a plague of humans upon the earth.

SECOND: POLLUTION. We must encourage people, through economic incentives and celebrity example, to use only zero-emission fuels. We must work toward total recycling of our consumer goods and consistent cleanup of our current pollution sites. We need to push for a scientific branch of government.

THIRD: TERRORISM. We must start the long and difficult job of getting a strong world government under the auspices of an overhauled UN. We must get a world court justice system, backed by a strong UN military and police force, up and running in the next five decades. We have to get international, ethnic, and religious conflict off the streets and battlefields and into the courtroom. We must move our animal aggression and our programmed need for war onto the sports fields. This is not impossible. We can do it.

I'm not saying that I expect the entire human race to suddenly switch from being an emotional animal to an objective caretaker in time to save this beautiful planet. But if we use our emotions, *as they are,* to motivate us to change our self-destructive patterns, there is still hope. With the assistance of financial incentives and celebrity leadership, we can use status and cognitive behavioral therapy to change the world's emotional attitude toward our biosphere from that of adversary to one of stewardship.

Time is of the essence. Yes, we are becoming more aware of our damage to the biosphere. The increased violence of our weather is getting our attention. However, we have already wasted four decades in denial. Until we can establish an accurate profile of who we are and why we are self-destructing, we will continue to dabble in denial. The longer we procrastinate, the more damage we will inflict on the biosphere. We are fiddling while the rain forests burn.

This has been *my* perspective on human destructiveness as seen through my belief system. Yours will be different. With enough points of view, we can establish a credible understanding of ourselves and our destructive behaviors. Your input is needed. The more points of view we can pull together, the more substance there will be to the promised wisdom from our human common consciousness. With thousands of outside perspectives, we can see what shakes out as the major behavioral and emotional roadblocks to understanding the damaging role we are playing in our over-stressed biosphere.

"In the end, our society will be defined not only by what we create, but by what we refuse to destroy."
— *John C. Sawhill*

Who do you think we are? Why do you think we are damaging our biosphere? What do you think we can do about it? Please send your theories, additions, corrections, or suggestions to:

Email:
gchism@mcn.org

Regular Mail:
Gordon Chism
P.O. Box 2184
Fort. Bragg, CA 95437

A Book List

Aronson, Elliot: *The Social Animal*
Crick, Francis: *The Astonishing Hypothesis*
Dennett, Daniel C.: *Consciousness Explained*
Doidge, Norman, M.D.: *The Brain That Changes Itself*
Giovannoli, Joseph: *The Biology of Belief*
Gladwell, Malcolm: *The Tipping Point*
Keirsey, David and Bates, Marilyn: *Please Understand Me*
LeDoux, Joseph: *The Emotional Brain*
LeDoux, Joseph: *Synaptic Self*
Marcus, Gary: *The Birth of the Mind*
Nohria, Lawrence: *Driven*
Pinker, Steven: *How the Mind Works*
Pinker, Steven: *The Blank Slate*
Tiger, Lionel and Fox, Robin: *The Imperial Animal*
Wilson, Edward O.: *Consilience*
Wilson, Edward O.: *On Human Nature*
Wilson, Edward O.: *Sociobiology*